FUNKY FOODS

FUNKY FOODS

Mix-and-Match Recipes to Feed
Kids With Food Allergies

12 Weeks of Rotation-Diet Menus

TRISHA SWINDLE

TATE PUBLISHING
AND ENTERPRISES, LLC

Published by Tate Publishing & Enterprises, LLC
127 E. Trade Center Terrace | Mustang, Oklahoma 73064 USA
1.888.361.9473 | www.tatepublishing.com

Tate Publishing is committed to excellence in the publishing industry. The company reflects the philosophy established by the founders, based on Psalm 68:11,
"The Lord gave the word and great was the company of those who published it."

Book design copyright © 2013 by Tate Publishing, LLC. All rights reserved.
Cover design by Nathan Harmony
Interior design by Mary Jean Archival

Published in the United States of America

ISBN: 978-1-61862-281-5
1. Cooking / Health & Healing / Allergy
2. Health & Fitness / Allergies
13.01.25

Table of Contents

Introduction

My middle child, Landon, was diagnosed with Eosinophilic Gastroenteritis (EG) at 15 months old. The fifteen months prior to this fancy-schmancy diagnosis were spent with me insisting that this otherwise healthy-looking infant was really, really sick. This does not bode well for convincing doctors to look at your child. It reminded me of taking a car into the mechanic—the car never makes the knocking sound for the mechanic. Landon would never have the same symptoms at the doctor's office that had him crying and waking up every one to three hours every night since the day he was born.

Very long story short—Landon had eosinophilic cells in his small intestines. Eosinophils are white blood cells found in everyone's blood. In people with eosinophilic diseases they are in places they shouldn't be or in larger numbers. Eos cells react to potential allergens. They are the cells that cause hives to form when you touch poison ivy. In Landon's digestive tract, these cells would overreact when he ate anything he was allergic to. The cells would then try to kill the vicious bad food and, in the process, his digestive tract. A host of bad things can happen if this isn't taken care of. Let's just say that no kid should ever have this condition. A cure at any time would be swell.

To help me with feeding the little dude, he has undergone numerous food allergy tests. One of the biggest challenges with this disease is that his food allergies change. He can be allergic to wheat and then six months later not be allergic to wheat. Not only do his food allergies change, but his list of allergens was typically so long that I stopped telling people what he couldn't eat and instead listed his safe foods. The next question was always, what *does* he eat?

I won't lie. I didn't start out making my own crackers, and serving quinoa for breakfast. In the beginning, Landon ate a very limited diet. Thankfully, we were still breastfeeding so I felt like I had some time to get my act together. But it was my mother-in-law, Carla who finally got me off my scared butt and into the kitchen. Every time she would watch the boys at her house I would bring Landon's food. And every visit she would open his lunch box and say, "Is this it?" to which I would force a smile and say, "Yup!" It was her next four words that finally hit hard: "You can do better."

She was right. For my child, I could do better. I spent an afternoon at a bookstore going through each and every allergy cookbook on the shelf. I trolled the Internet and harassed the nutritionist at the pediatric gastroenterologist's office. I walked up to complete strangers at the "hippie dippie" grocery store and asked them what they were going to do with whatever odd-looking produce they had in their cart.

Slowly, but surely I put together food Landon could eat. I learned how to bake my own granola bars, read food labels for hidden allergens, and pack every bite he took with nutrition. Even if he couldn't eat "normal" food, I didn't want him missing out on how fun food could be, or suffering from the nutritional holes that a restricted diet can leave. Where do you find calcium when you can't drink milk? If he's not eating much meat (because he was a toot) what sort of nutrients is he missing and where do I find a substitute?

Once I got my cooking feet underneath me, and Landon started sleeping through the night, I launched Funky Food Allergies as an online resource to help other parents coping with food allergies. This was also a place for me to talk about the frustrations and joys of living with a child with multiple food allergies. The recipes you will find here and online at funkyfoodallergies.blogspot.com, fit a few simple criteria.

I wanted recipes anyone could easily tailor to fit their own allergen needs. They had to be simple—life is too short to spend two hours stirring a pot. Finally, they had to be delicious and fun. Kids with food allergies still need to enjoy their food!

This is important, because I wanted these recipes to be something any busy person could easily add to their lives. Most of the recipes are also vegan or vegetarian, simply because Landon was allergic to most of the same ingredients those specialized eaters avoid. Plus, all these recipes use whole, nutritious ingredients, something that any family trying to eat a healthier diet can add to their pantry with confidence.

I have also included three months of a three-day rotation diet menu. Rotation diets can be a life-saver for a child with severe food allergies. I finally broke down and did this with Landon when he was at his worst. Rotation diets can be daunting. I hope having these menus to pull from will help! You will find either the original recipe in the cookbook or directions on where to find it. More on Rotation Diets in a minute.

What do Landon and the rest of my family eat? Tons of fantastic, delicious, and most of all truly, Funky Food!

A word of caution: I am a mom, not a doctor. Please consult your physician before making any changes to your child's diet.

Where to Begin?

So you've been handed this mixed bag of a diagnosis that include allergies to foods. Now what? I remember looking through the first allergy cookbook I was handed and not making it past a soup that involved over three hours of babysitting on the stovetop. There was no way I was going to be able to do that with two kids under three. I could barely make it through a complete shower without someone needing me! After I threw that cookbook back at the bookshelf I found it on, I felt so defeated. Where did I start? There was the ever present thought that failure was not an option—Landon's very survival was counting on my ability to feed him. As dramatic as that sounds, we all know that feeling. So breathe. Make one change at a time. Find the processed foods your child can eat and regardless of the expense use those at first, while getting your cooking feet under you. Then slowly one by one, add a new recipe into your life. Before long you'll find yourself baking things you had never dreamed. Happily (okay, mostly) providing a healthy, balanced diet for your family.

Starting Suggestions

Recipes:

The place I would recommend starting in this book is either the Super Smoothie or the Granola Bars. These two recipes are very simple but go a long way towards filling tummies. They are portable which is also huge in saving your sanity.

Ingredients:

Of course remove anything your child is allergic to, but if you have ingredients that your child is intolerant too, you might want to slowly remove it. For instance, Landon's older brother Brenden is dairy intolerant but *loved* his milk. So instead of handing him a glass of rice milk and hoping for the best, I slowly weaned him from the dairy. The first glass was 75 percent dairy and 25 percent rice milk until one day it was 100 percent rice milk.

Gadgets:

The priority of gadget purchase depends on what ingredients you have lost and what foods are important to your child. For us, losing wheat was the hardest—we really missed bread! So the first new toy I purchased was the bread machine.

Funky Ingredients

I vaguely remember life before I knew the correct pronunciation for quinoa (FYI, not pronounced *kee-no-ah* but *keen-wah*). It was a simpler time when the only two grains in my life were wheat and rice. This may have been simpler, but there are numerous advantages to cooking and baking with a variety of grains. They have different tastes, textures, and most are packed with nutrients kiddos with food allergies are missing in their restricted diets. But grains aren't the only new ingredients that found their way into my cupboard. This is a brief guide to the funky ingredients you will find in this cookbook and in regular rotation in my kitchen.

Flours

Almond

Almond meal is a great way to add a nutritional boost to just about any recipe calling for flour. Almond meal is packed with Vitamin E, calcium, fiber, protein and Omega 3s. Yum! It's also low in carbohydrates. Simply add in about 1/4 cup of almond meal to replace a portion of flour. For a real almond delight, check out the Almond Cookies (page 215)!

Amaranth

Amaranth is a nutritional powerhouse. It's loaded with fiber, calcium, and iron. More importantly, though, it is one of the few non-meat sources of balanced protein. This is another one of those ingredients that can really fill in the nutritional gaps in a child's restricted diet. It has a wonderful nutty flavor that lends well to bread, pancakes, and muffins.

Buckwheat

You have not truly lived until you have tried 100 percent buckwheat pancakes. They are—well, I need to go make some now. That's how good they are. This nutty flavored flour is chock full of magnesium which is good for healthy hearts, so definitely add some to your plate too! High in insoluble fiber and manganese, this one also contains eight of the essential amino acids, making it a great replacement for meats. Beyond the pancakes, buckwheat makes great cookies, crackers, and coating for fish or chicken nuggets!

Carob

Carob is the one legume flour I like to cook with. It is what you grab when you need a little "chocolate" boost sans the chocolate. Not that there is anything wrong with chocolate, but it was on Landon's "no" list for a while, and a mom can't ask their child to give up chocolate without a decent replacement! Carob is also a great source of calcium, potassium, copper, manganese, and fiber. The only drawback is that it is high in sugar, so use it sparingly in muffins, pancakes, cookies, and cakes.

Millet

Millet flour can be hard to find so don't shy away from grinding your own—a Vitamix or food processor work great. It doesn't have to be perfectly smooth in order to work fine in these recipes. Millet is a great source of manganese, fiber, B vitamins, magnesium, and phosphorus. It's also loaded with essential amino acids making it a good protein source. I love using millet as a coating for fish or meats (it makes a chicken nugget look just like the ones from the grocery store!). Millet can be somewhat dry, so I like using it in recipes that are already moist, like the Irish Soda Bread. It's also good in crackers and breads!

Oat

Oats sometimes get a bad rap in the gluten-free world. The question goes back and forth are they or aren't they gluten-free? Let me help you out. They are gluten-free, have always been gluten-free, will always be gluten-free. The problem lies in the manufacturing process. Frequently they are processed on the same equipment that processes wheat, so they can become contaminated with gluten. This is why you should only buy oats that are certified gluten-free. So don't hate the oats. They are wonderful! This is another flour packed with magnesium, phosphorus, Vitamin B1, fiber, and protein. Oat flour is incredibly moist, so in substitutions use three parts oat flour and one part dry flour (millet or rice). It makes the most amazing cupcakes—so good, in fact, that I bet your child's classmates won't be able to tell the difference!

Quinoa

I had a hard time coming to love quinoa flour. It has a really strong flavor. I mean really, really strong. I love the grain but as a flour, it was hard for me to find a place for it. In small portions—a quarter cup or less—it is a wonderful way to enrich your flour blends. As the majority ingredient it makes fantastic crackers. This flour is worth having in your pantry as it's a good source of manganese, fiber, iron, copper, magnesium, phosphorus, and essential amino acids (EAA). These precious EAA's are what makes quinoa a great way to get a balanced protein in a non-meat source.

Rice

I am not the biggest fan of rice flour—it tends to be gritty and dry. Plus it's not a dense source of nutrients. My favorite place to use it is in my Oat Flour Cupcakes (page 222). The moist qualities of the oat flour need a dry flour to balance, and rice works perfect! Rice flour is a good source of protein, fiber, and manganese.

Sorghum

Sorghum isn't a nutrition powerhouse, but it's a moister flour than rice so I find it more versatile. It does have a decent amount of fiber and protein and works great in muffins, cakes, and cookies. It has a mild nutty flavor.

Starches

These are the three starches I use the most often:

- Arrowroot
- Potato
- Tapioca

There are other options, but for the sake of brevity we'll stick to these three. They all perform about the same and are used for the same reasons—they help give gluten-free (GF) flours some stick-togetherness. GF flours tend to be dry and crumbly; a starch is used to help keep the baked good moist. They are also fantastic thickeners in things like stir-fries or sauces. Nutritionally there isn't anything interesting about starches so I'm going to skip it.

Teff

I started baking with Teff when Landon was on the rotation diet. It works great in muffins and cakes. I love that it's a great source of protein, fiber, calcium, copper, and iron. It's a dark colored grain so I find it works great in pumpkin breads or gingerbread muffins.

Miscellaneous

Essential Amino Acids

This isn't so much an ingredient as an important part of an ingredient. Kids on restricted diets or just a good 'ol fashioned picky eater will have holes in their diet. At one point Landon wasn't a big fan of most meats and was allergic to soy, so this left fewer choices for protein sources. The reason this was significant was essential amino acids (EAA). These tiny little boogers are necessary for a laundry list of really important tasks in your body. Everything from building cells and repairing tissue to forming antibodies that help keep you healthy are done by EAA's. Most American's get their essential amino acids from meat, but if you can't eat meat, no worries, here are my favorite Funky Food EAA sources:

- Brewer's Yeast
- Quinoa

But it's such a short list! There are tons of Funky Food friendly almost-complete protein sources that when combined together give you a complete protein. Such as:

- Nut Butters and Buckwheat Crackers
- Peas and Brown Rice
- Hempseeds in a Millet Muffin

Essential Fatty Acids

Americans in general don't eat enough essential fatty acids (EFA) so we all need to add these superheroes of the nutrition world to our diets. EFA's reduce inflammation, promote brain development, and keep your heart healthy. Unlike essential amino acids, these are really simple to add into your diet—no need to be concerned about "complete" forms. There are three omega-3 essential fatty acids that we all need. I'm going to spare you the ridiculously long scientific words and simply use the abbreviations: ALA, DHA, and EPA. ALA is a snap to find in the Funky Food world but the other two can only be found in oily, cold water fish such as herrings or salmon. I use a fish oil supplement for my family. Make sure the supplement is molecularly distilled to prevent any mercury from getting into your munchkins. These are my favorite Funky Food friendly EFA sources:

- Nordic Naturals Baby or Children's Cod Liver Oil (DHA/EPA)
- Hempseeds (ALA)
- Flaxseeds (ALA)
- Nuts/Seeds (ALA)

Hulled Hemp Seeds

Hemp is not the same thing as marijuana—let's get that out of the way first off. If you use hemp seeds or hemp milk there will be no munchies, paranoia, or a predilection to the word "dude." Hemp is in the same botanical family as marijuana, but hemp is as different from pot as rice is from wheat. Make sense? I use hulled hemp seeds in my baked goods and even meatballs because they provide a great dose of omega 3 fatty acids and protein. They have a very mild taste and are so tiny that they don't change the texture of what they are put in. Hulled hemp seeds also make a great seed butter—perfect for non-peanut or tree nut PBJs!

Xantham Gum

Well, I could go into the science behind the magic that is xantham gum but I'm going to go ahead and assume that you are probably a bit sleep deprived and frankly have more interesting things to ponder. The short version is that it's part of a bacterial coating of a really long scientific term. It does contain corn but in small amounts. Landon didn't react to it, but be careful if you or your child is allergic to corn. Xantham gum is used to thicken (sauces) or to bind flours together. It replaces gluten in gluten-free products.

It's what makes your gluten-free bread more like bread and less like baked flour. Don't let the price tag scare you—most recipes only call for half a teaspoon, so that precious bag o' xantham gum will last a long, long, long time.

Funky Ingredient Sources

Because, let's be honest, most of these ingredients are not found in your average grocery store. You have options though, the first being developing a relationship with online purchasing. There are three gazillion websites out that sell all these ingredients. One of my favorites is Vitacost.com—they've been around for a while and have secure purchasing available, both of which are important for that gooey feeling of trust you need when tossing your credit card information into the great, vast internet.

The second is a trick that I learned during my brief stint as a Whole Foods employee is that all products found in a grocery store are purchased through a distributor. Distributors give grocery stores these huge lists of products that they have available to sell. So call the company that makes one of your favorite products and find out who their distributor is in your area. Then contact your grocery store and see if they would be willing to order it for you, to either, A: keep on their shelves or B: allow you to buy a case of it. This is significant because you won't pay for shipping and frequently you can negotiate a discount if you buy a case of it. If the product is something that spoils quickly and can't be stored long (in the freezer), then find a group and see if they would be willing to split a case. This can also be a great opportunity to find other families living on Funky Food! Giving your kiddos a chance to make friends with other munchkins living with foods allergies.

Gadgets

Gadgets aren't necessary to cook Funky Food but they sure make it easier. When you are producing food that most people simply buy, like crackers, you need to help yourself out in any way you can. So invest in a few good kitchen tools! You deserve it!

Blender

I'm not going to lie, I love my Vitamix. But I inherited it from a friend (Thanks April!), so I'm not sure my love would extend if I had had to drop the money on it. This bad boy of blenders can pulverize almost anything! My second recommendation is the Bullet. It does short work on smoothies and making fruit/veggie purees. It's a snap to clean and store. I am not a huge fan of a traditional blender as they require too much babysitting to get them to grind grains or puree veggies.

Bread Machine

It is really, really hard to make gluten-free bread without a bread machine. GF dough tends to be really sticky and wet, and adding more flour to make it non-sticky will result in a loaf that you could use as a doorstop. My favorite bread machine is the Breadman TR875 Bread Machine. This one has a gluten-free cycle! Definitely worth it. You can find this online or at your favorite appliance store.

Food Processor

This is a gadget worth spending a little money on. You will use it for making breadcrumbs, nut/seed butters, fruit/veggie purees, and so much more. Love me some Kitchen Aid products.

Nut/Seed Milk Maker

You can buy almost any nut/seed milk these days but you will save yourself quite a few dollars if you make it yourself, and this machine will make it easy. There are a few brands on the market but the one I use is the Soyabella. You toss in your nuts/seeds and some water and press start! This machine came in very handy when we were doing the rotation diet. I could make just what we needed instead of having to throw out or freeze extra nut/seed milk. So nice! Although every appliance store should sell these, I have only found them online.

Rice Maker

Trust me, take the six bucks you would have spent on the venti latte from your favorite coffee shop and go buy a rice maker. It will save you a ton of time and worry over watching the pot of rice on your stovetop. Plus you can cook quinoa, millet, and buckwheat in it as well. For a perfect easy breakfast for busy mornings, just toss the grain of choice in the rice maker, add water, and go finish getting ready. By the time you're gorgeous, the pot of quinoa will be ready to dish up to a table full of waiting munchkins.

Silicone Bakeware

This stuff rocks. At the very least, get the liners for your baking sheets. Using silicone bakeware keeps you from having to butter or oil a baking sheet or mold. This may not seem like a huge deal until you only have one very specific fat to choose from and it doesn't grease baking sheets well! No longer the elite world belonging only to the French Company "Silpat", every baking supply company makes their own version, available practically everywhere.

Stainless Steel Drink Containers

I love the insulated ones. They keep Super Smoothies cold and portable. This was incredibly important when I was trying to get every calorie I could into Landon. They will save you time and money because you won't be stopping to buy drinks and then spend ten minutes reading labels until you find the one thing your child can drink.

Surviving in the Great Big World

You cleared out the pantry, you've started using ingredients you can barely pronounce and baking things you didn't know could be produced without the help of some large company. You've made your house safe for your kiddo but what about the rest of the world looming outside your front door? I would love to tell you that everyone you meet is going to truly comprehend the importance of preventing your child from coming into contact with a food they are allergic too. But I can't. Even people who care about Landon tremendously, and want to do right by his allergies simply don't get it. These are are a few ways to help your child navigate a world filled with food that I have found work!

First Line of Defense

This is your child. Hopefully they will grow out of their allergies but it is likely that this may be part of their life for a very long time. Start talking about allergies as soon as you get a diagnosis, even if your little one isn't talking yet. Make this a simple part of their life in the same way you explain rules about holding hands when crossing the street. It doesn't have to be weird or even scary to your child. One way to do this is to point out your own allergies or the allergies of another adult. My husband and I both have a few food allergies. I'm allergic to shellfish and Andrew is allergic to plums (weird, huh?). So when we are at restaurants or even at our own table, should those ingredients appear, we talk about them. Landon thinks it's awesome that he can eat shrimp and Mommy can't. He giggles when he eats plums and Daddy can't. This really helps when he feels left out or frustrated by his restrictions.

Landon gets horrible tummy aches when he eats something he's reacting too. We talk about these reactions. This way when he's at school and someone offers him a cupcake, he remembers the tummy ache he had the last time he ate wheat and will pass on the cupcake. So talk about what sort of things will happen to your child if they choose to eat something they shouldn't. Also remind them what steps they need to take if they start having a reaction.

School

This has by far been the hardest one for me to date. I'm sure when Landon becomes a teenager or moves out on his own will be harder but handing him over to another adult was plain, ol' fashioned terrifying. Asking a few questions and supplying plenty of information will help keep your munchkin safe.

Questions to ask:

1. Who will be teaching/watching my child? You will meet his/her main teacher but I guarantee there are multiple people who will actually be caring for your child throughout the day that you will never see or hear of. Teacher aides at lunch or recess time, a Music or PE teacher and many, many more. Each one of these people need to be familiar with your child's allergies.

2. Is there a Registered Nurse on site?

3. Do all employees have First Aid/CPR training?

4. Does your facility have experience with food allergies?

5. What sorts of precautions are taken?

Steps to take:

1. Get your child a Medical Alert ID. These come in tons of great forms; bracelets, tags for shoelaces, necklaces, etc. The designs are also fun! This does not have to be a boring piece of jewelry, let your kiddo pick one out that appeals to them and they will be more likely to wear it.

2. Have stickers printed up. When Landon was under 5, I had stickers printed up that had a warning about his food allergies. Then on his way out the door, I would slap one on the back of his shoulder. This way a substitute would easily see it and know to ask about his food allergies. I also placed one on his lunch box.

3. Print off a simple form with your child's allergies and any steps that need to be taken to keep him/her safe, like an EPI Pen and its' location. Laminate it and ask your child's school for several places to post it. This will reduce the chances that a volunteer or substitute won't be told about your child's allergies.

4. Offer to host an education workshop on food allergies for the staff or the families of the school.

Remember, you are going to encounter people who refuse to work with your child's allergies or who just don't get it. Never be afraid to advocate for your child or that you are over-reacting. For some children the room for mistakes is miniscule so do what you think is best.

Rotation Diets/Menus

I had read about Rotation Diets a little when I first started dealing with Landon's food allergies, but I have to admit that it sounded complicated and adding more restrictions to an already restricted diet seemed unduly cruel. It wasn't until he started reacting to new foods with each allergy test that I finally reached for the Rotation Diet. It was the allergy test that we lost amaranth, sunflower seeds, and flaxseeds that I realized simply removing new allergic foods wasn't going to work for Landon. His digestive tract and immune system needed a break only a Rotation Diet could provide.

Why Use a Rotation Diet?

The idea here is to not allow antibodies the chance to build up. By the time a food is reintroduced the immune system will have forgotten about it. This can help give digestive tracts like Landon's a chance to heal existing damage. It will also help the immune system to "forget" the foods it is allergic to—the goal being no bad immune responses to food.

Feeding the Family:

I am not a short order cook. I like to cook, don't get me wrong, but I do not long for a day spent poking my head in the dining room inquiring, "And what will you be having this evening?" to my loving family members. So, my plan was to continue doing what we are already doing, which was to feed everyone a modified version of Landon's diet. If I make enchiladas I add corn (a "no" ingredient for him) to the mixture after I make Landon's batch.

Rotation Diet 101:

Each food is part of a biological and botanical family. In a rotation diet you eat one food, say wheat on Day 1 but not again until Day 4. First cousins—foods that are in the same family are to be eaten on alternating days; so wheat on Day 1 and then rice on Day 3. Are you with me? I could include an enormous list of all the botanical and biological food families but I'm really, really lazy. You can find these complete lists online by searching: botanical/biological food families.

You can choose to omit all the foods your child is reacting too or only the worst offenders. For instance, I chose to rotate all ingredients in Landon's diet except for wheat, soy, corn, eggs, and dairy (cow). These were the foods that caused the worst reactions for him. Watch your child carefully if you are using foods that have caused reaction. Although while doing a rotation diet, they shouldn't have a reaction to a food, immune systems aren't always told these things. As with all things food allergy related, please consult your doctor before starting.

Funky Food Rotation Diet Tips:

I bought a dry erase calendar to write out my weekly rotation diet menu. Across the top I listed the days of the week; down the left side was the meals.

First, I pick my ingredients. I found it was easier to match meals around ingredients than the other way around. Each day had:

- Fruit

- Grain

- Meat

- Milk

- Oil
- Sweetener
- Vegetable

Tip: Choose one favorite food per day; this can help keep everyone happier about the rules!

Then I pick recipes that fit the ingredients. There are some ingredients that pair together gorgeously. For instance millet rocks in the Irish Soda Bread but makes awful pancakes; where as buckwheat makes great pancakes. This also helps make some "no brainer" options, a great blessing for a sleep-deprived mom. In the Rotation Diet Menus that follow, I have chosen ingredients that work well for the recipes in this cookbook. If one of the ingredients I use is on your child's "no" list, try to choose a replacement that is a first cousin botanically. This will make it fit into the rotation diet easier.

Explaining this to a child or a caregiver is a challenge. To make this easier, I also purchased several same sized containers that I could easily label for holding dry goods like crackers. Then I labeled one for every day of the week, making it easier to feed him. All a caregiver would have to do is grab the Monday container and hand him a handful of whatever was in it for a snack. I would write up a copy of the week's meal plan and post it on the fridge. By far the weirdest part of my rotation diet experience was explaining to Landon why he had to eat apples on Apple Day instead of the pears he wanted!

This gets easier after a few weeks so hang in there!

Week 1
Monday

- Fruit: Grapes
- Grain: Teff
- Meat: Turkey
- Milk: Hemp
- Oil: Hemp
- Sweetener: Agave Nectar
- Vegetable: Zucchini

- Breakfast: Teff Muffins
- Snack: Grapes and Macadamia Nuts
- Lunch: Deli Turkey, Grapes, and Teff Bread
- Snack: Hemp Pudding
- Dinner: Turkey Meatballs, Zucchini, and Grapes

Tuesday

- Fruit: Apple
- Grain: Buckwheat
- Meat: Chicken
- Milk: Almond
- Oil: Almond
- Sweetener: Honey
- Vegetable: Broccoli

- Breakfast: Buckwheat Pancakes
- Snack: Apples and Almonds
- Lunch: Chicken Hotdogs, Applesauce, and Buckwheat Bread
- Snack: Apples with Almond Butter
- Dinner: Chicken Strips, Broccoli, and Apples

Wednesday

- Fruit: Strawberries
- Grain: Rice
- Meat: Beef
- Milk: Rice
- Oil: Olive
- Sweetener: Brown Rice Syrup
- Vegetable: Peas

- Breakfast: Rice with Cinnamon and Brown Rice syrup
- Snack: Strawberry Smoothie
- Lunch: Rice Crackers, Pecan Butter, Strawberries and Peas
- Snack: Rice Yogurt
- Dinner: Beef and Rice, Peas, and Strawberries

Thursday

- Fruit: Oranges
- Grain: Amaranth
- Meat: Fish
- Milk: Cashew
- Oil: Safflower
- Sweetener: Maple Syrup
- Vegetable: Potatoes

- Breakfast: Amaranth Pancakes
- Snack: Oranges dipped in Chocolate
- Lunch: Amaranth Bread, Cashew Butter, and Oranges
- Snack: Amaranth Crackers with Cashew Butter
- Dinner: Fish, French Fries, and Oranges

Friday

- Fruit: Pears and Cranberries
- Grain: Sorghum
- Meat: Chicken
- Milk: Almond
- Oil: Almond
- Sweetener: Honey
- Vegetable: Green Beans

- Breakfast: Sorghum Muffins
- Snack: Almonds and Dried Cranberries
- Lunch: Chicken Salad, Pears, and Sorghum Bread
- Snack: Sorghum Muffins
- Dinner: Chicken Salad, Green Beans, and Pears

Saturday

- Fruit: Apples
- Grain: Quinoa
- Meat: Turkey
- Milk: Coconut
- Oil: Coconut
- Sweetener: Agave Nectar
- Vegetable: Asparagus

- Breakfast: Toasted Quinoa Flakes
- Snack: Walnuts and Apples
- Lunch: Quinoa Crackers, Walnut Butter, and Apples
- Snack: Coconut Yogurt
- Dinner: Turkey Meatloaf, Asparagus, and Apples

Sunday

- Fruit: Grapes
- Grain: Rice
- Meat: Beef
- Milk: Rice
- Oil: Macadamia
- Sweetener: Brown Rice Syrup
- Vegetable: Broccoli

- Breakfast: Rice with Cinnamon and Sugar
- Snack: Macadamia Nuts and Grapes
- Lunch: Beef Hotdogs, Grapes, and Rice Yogurt
- Snack: Rice Pudding
- Dinner: Beef Hotdogs, Grapes, and Broccoli

Week 2

Monday

- Fruit: Strawberries
- Grain: Amaranth
- Meat: Fish
- Milk: Almond
- Oil: Almond
- Sweetener: Maple Syrup
- Vegetable: Sweet Potato

- Breakfast: Amaranth Muffins
- Snack: Almond Cookies
- Lunch: Almond Butter, Amaranth Crackers, and Strawberries
- Snack: Almond Cookies
- Dinner: Fish, Sweet Potato Oven Fries, and Strawberries

Tuesday

- Fruit: Oranges
- Grain: Buckwheat
- Meat: Lamb
- Milk: Cashew
- Oil: Cashew
- Sweetener: Agave
- Vegetable: Zucchini

- Breakfast: Buckwheat Pancakes
- Snack: Cashews and Oranges
- Lunch: Cashew Butter, Oranges, and Buckwheat Bread
- Snack: Buckwheat Pancakes
- Dinner: Lamb Roast, Zucchini, and Oranges

Wednesday

- Fruit: Apples
- Grain: Sorghum
- Meat: Turkey
- Milk: Hemp
- Oil: Hemp
- Sweetener: Cane Sugar
- Vegetable: Green Beans

- Breakfast: Sorghum Pancakes
- Snack: Hemp Butter and Sorghum Crackers
- Lunch: Deli Turkey, Apples, and Sorghum Crackers
- Snack: Hazelnuts and Apples
- Dinner: Turkey Chili, Green Beans, and Apples

Thursday

- Fruit: Blueberries
- Grain: Quinoa
- Meat: Beef
- Milk: Pumpkin Seed
- Oil: Canola
- Sweetener: Maple Syrup
- Vegetable: Broccoli

- Breakfast: Quinoa with Cinnamon and Sugar
- Snack: Pumpkin Seeds and Dried Blueberries
- Lunch: Quinoa Salad with Peas and Blueberries
- Snack: Pumpkin Seed, Milk, and Yogurt
- Dinner: Hamburgers, Broccoli, and Blueberries

Friday

- Fruit: Pears
- Grain: Millet
- Meat: Chicken
- Milk: Almond
- Oil: Almond
- Sweetener: Agave
- Vegetable: Asparagus

- Breakfast: Millet with Cinnamon and Sugar
- Snack: Macadamia Nuts
- Lunch: Chicken Hotdogs, Pears, and Almond Meal Crackers
- Snack: Millet Pudding
- Dinner: Chicken Hotdogs, Pears, and Asparagus

Saturday

- Fruit: Grapes
- Grain: Buckwheat
- Meat: Fish
- Milk: Coconut
- Oil: Coconut
- Sweetener: Stevia
- Vegetable: Potato

- Breakfast: Buckwheat Pancakes
- Snack: Coconut Milk Yogurt
- Lunch: Pecan Butter Balls, Grapes, and Buckwheat Crackers
- Snack: Buckwheat Cookies
- Dinner: Fish, French Fries, and Grapes

Sunday

- Fruit: Banana
- Grain: Rice
- Meat: Turkey
- Milk: Rice
- Oil: Pumpkin Seed
- Sweetener: Brown Rice Syrup
- Vegetable: Pumpkin

- Breakfast: Rice with Brown Rice Syrup and Cinnamon
- Snack: Pumpkin Seeds and Dried Cranberries
- Lunch: Deli Turkey, Rice Crackers, and Apples
- Snack: Pumpkin Seeds and Dried Cranberries
- Dinner: Turkey Meatballs, Banana, and Mashed Pumpkin

Week 3

Monday

- Fruit: Blueberries
- Grain: Carob
- Meat: Pork
- Milk: Hemp
- Oil: Hemp
- Sweetener: Maple Syrup
- Vegetable: Green Beans

- Breakfast: Carob Pancakes
- Snack: Hazelnuts and Dried Blueberries
- Lunch: Hemp Butter, Carob Crackers, and Blueberries
- Snack: Hazelnuts and Dried Blueberries
- Dinner: Sliced Ham, Green Beans, and Blueberries

Tuesday

- Fruit: Apples
- Grain: Rice
- Meat: Chicken
- Milk: Rice
- Oil: Almond
- Sweetener: Brown Rice Syrup
- Vegetable: Broccoli

- Breakfast: Rice with Dried Apples and Cinnamon
- Snack: Almonds
- Lunch: Deli Chicken Breast, Apples, and Rice Crackers
- Snack: Almond Cookies
- Dinner: Chicken Soup, Apples, and Broccoli

Wednesday

- Fruit: Strawberries
- Grain: Buckwheat
- Meat: Meat Free Day
- Milk: Cashew
- Oil: Cashew
- Sweetener: Agave
- Vegetable: Zucchini

- Breakfast: Buckwheat Pancakes
- Snack: Cashews and Dried Cranberries
- Lunch: Buckwheat Crackers, Cashew Butter, and Strawberries
- Snack: Cashews and Dried Cranberries
- Dinner: Buckwheat Pasta, Strawberries, and Zucchini

Thursday

- Fruit: Grapes
- Grain: Quinoa
- Meat: Fish
- Milk: Macadamia
- Oil: Macadamia
- Sweetener: Stevia
- Vegetable: Sweet Potato

- Breakfast: Quinoa with Cinnamon and Raisins
- Snack: Macadamia Nuts
- Lunch: Macadamia Nut Butter, Quinoa Crackers, Grapes, and Sweet Potato Chips
- Snack: Quinoa Pudding
- Dinner: Fish, Sweet Potato Oven Fries, and Grapes

Friday

- Fruit: Oranges
- Grain: Teff
- Meat: Turkey
- Milk: Coconut
- Oil: Coconut
- Sweetener: Cane Sugar
- Vegetable: Parsnips

- Breakfast: Coconut Pancakes
- Snack: Walnuts
- Lunch: Sliced Turkey, Teff Crackers, and Oranges
- Snack: Coconut Milk Yogurt
- Dinner: Roast Turkey Breast, Parsnips, and Oranges

Saturday

- Fruit: Pineapple
- Grain: Almond Meal
- Meat: Beef
- Milk: Almond
- Oil: Almond
- Sweetener: Agave
- Vegetable: Asparagus

- Breakfast: Almond Meal Pancakes
- Snack: Almonds and Dried Blueberries
- Lunch: Almond Crackers, Almond Butter, and Pineapple
- Snack: Almond Cookies
- Dinner: Meatballs, Asparagus, and Pineapple

Sunday

- Fruit: Pears
- Grain: Millet
- Meat: Chicken
- Milk: Pumpkin Seed
- Oil: Pumpkin Seed
- Sweetener: Maple Syrup
- Vegetable: Potato

- Breakfast: Millet with Cinnamon and Maple Syrup
- Snack: Pumpkin Seeds
- Lunch: Chicken Hotdogs, Millet Crackers, Pears
- Snack: Millet Pudding
- Dinner: Chicken Hotdogs, French Fries, Pears

Week 4

Monday

- Fruit: Strawberries
- Grain: Buckwheat
- Meat: Meat Free Day
- Milk: Cashew
- Oil: Cashew
- Sweetener: Honey
- Vegetable: Squash

- Breakfast: Buckwheat Pancakes
- Snack: Cashews
- Lunch: Buckwheat Crackers, Cashew Butter, and Strawberries
- Snack: Cashews and Dried Strawberries
- Dinner: Buckwheat Pasta, Baked Squash, and Strawberries

Tuesday

- Fruit: Blackberry
- Grain: Sorghum
- Meat: Fish
- Milk: Hemp
- Oil: Hemp
- Sweetener: Cane Sugar
- Vegetable: Potato

- Breakfast: Sorghum Muffins
- Snack: Macadamia Nuts
- Lunch: Sorghum Crackers, Hemp Butter, and Blackberry
- Snack: Hemp Yogurt
- Dinner: Fish, French Fries, and Blackberry

Wednesday

- Fruit: Blueberries
- Grain: Quinoa
- Meat: Turkey
- Milk: Almond
- Oil: Almond
- Sweetener: Maple Syrup
- Vegetable: Cauliflower

- Breakfast: Quinoa
- Snack: Almonds and Dried Blueberries
- Lunch: Deli Turkey, Quinoa Crackers, and Blueberries
- Snack: Almond Cookies
- Dinner: Turkey Hotdogs, Baked Cauliflower, and Blueberries

Thursday

- Fruit: Apple
- Grain: Oat
- Meat: Beef
- Milk: Oat
- Oil: Hazelnut
- Sweetener: Cane Sugar
- Vegetable: Asparagus

- Breakfast: Oatmeal
- Snack: Hazelnuts
- Lunch: Hazelnut Butter, Oat Crackers, and Apples
- Snack: Oatmeal Cookies
- Dinner: Meatballs, Asparagus, and Apples

Friday

- Fruit: Grapes
- Grain: Carob
- Meat: Chicken
- Milk: Coconut
- Oil: Coconut
- Sweetener: Honey
- Vegetable: Asparagus

- Breakfast: Carob and Coconut Pancakes
- Snack: Pecans and Raisins
- Lunch: Pecan Butter, Carob Crackers, and Grapes
- Snack: Coconut Milk Yogurt
- Dinner: Baked Coconut Chicken Breasts, Peas, and Grapes

Saturday

- Fruit: Banana
- Grain: Millet
- Meat: Pork
- Milk: Hemp
- Oil: Hemp
- Sweetener: Maple Syrup
- Vegetable: Potato

- Breakfast: Millet
- Snack: Walnuts and Dried Cranberries
- Lunch: Deli Ham, Millet Crackers, and Banana
- Snack: Millet Pudding
- Dinner: Pork Chops, Mashed Potatoes, and Banana

Sunday

- Fruit: Oranges
- Grain: Buckwheat
- Meat: Turkey
- Milk: Coconut
- Oil: Coconut
- Sweetener: Agave
- Vegetable: Broccoli

- Breakfast: Buckwheat Pancakes
- Snack: Brazil Nuts
- Lunch: Brazil Nut Butter, Buckwheat Crackers, and Oranges
- Snack: Deli Turkey and Buckwheat Crackers
- Dinner: Turkey Breast, Broccoli, and Oranges

Week 5

Monday

- Fruit: Strawberries
- Grain: Quinoa
- Meat: Fish
- Milk: Coconut
- Oil: Coconut
- Sweetener: Honey
- Vegetable: Green Beans

- Breakfast: Quinoa
- Snack: Pecans
- Lunch: Quinoa Crackers, Pecan Butter, and Strawberries
- Snack: Coconut Milk Yogurt
- Dinner: Quinoa Flake/Coconut Fish, Green Beans, and Strawberries

Tuesday

- Fruit: Pineapple
- Grain: Oatmeal
- Meat: Chicken
- Milk: Oat
- Oil: Hazelnut
- Sweetener: Beet Sugar
- Vegetable: Asparagus

- Breakfast: Oatmeal

- Snack: Hazelnuts

- Lunch: Deli Chicken, Oat Crackers, and Pineapple

- Snack: Oatmeal Cookies

- Dinner: Chicken Nuggets, Asparagus, and Pineapple

Wednesday

- Fruit: Blueberries

- Grain: Quinoa

- Meat: Turkey

- Milk: Almond

- Oil: Almond

- Sweetener: Maple Syrup

- Vegetable: Cauliflower

- Breakfast: Quinoa with Cinnamon and Maple Syrup

- Snack: Almonds and Dried Blueberries

- Lunch: Quinoa Crackers, Almond Butter, and Blueberries

- Snack: Almond Pudding

- Dinner: Roasted Turkey Breast, Baked Cauliflower, and Blueberries

Thursday

- Fruit: Apple
- Grain: Buckwheat
- Meat: Lamb
- Milk: Coconut
- Oil: Coconut
- Sweetener: Agave
- Vegetable: Peas

- Breakfast: Buckwheat Pancakes
- Snack: Macadamia Nuts
- Lunch: Buckwheat Crackers, Macadamia Nut Butter, and Apples
- Snack: Coconut Milk Yogurt
- Dinner: Roast Lamb, Peas, and Apples

Friday

- Fruit: Grapes
- Grain: Millet
- Meat: Lamb
- Milk: Almond
- Oil: Almond
- Sweetener: Honey
- Vegetable: Broccoli

- Breakfast: Irish Soda Bread
- Snack: Almonds and Raisins
- Lunch: Deli Turkey, Millet Crackers, and Grapes
- Snack: Almond Butter and Millet Crackers
- Dinner: BBQ Shredded Turkey Sandwiches, Broccoli, and Grapes

Saturday

- Fruit: Orange
- Grain: Oatmeal
- Meat: Fish
- Milk: Cashew
- Oil: Cashew
- Sweetener: Beet Sugar
- Vegetable: Sweet Potato

- Breakfast: Oatmeal
- Snack: Cashews
- Lunch: Oat Crackers, Cashew Butter, and Oranges
- Snack: Oatmeal Cookies
- Dinner: Baked Fish, Sweet Potato Fries, and Orange

Sunday

- Fruit: Blackberries
- Grain: Quinoa
- Meat: Chicken
- Milk: Hemp
- Oil: Hemp
- Sweetener: Stevia
- Vegetable: Green Beans

- Breakfast: Quinoa
- Snack: Brazil Nuts
- Lunch: Deli Chicken, Quinoa Crackers, and Blackberries
- Snack: Quinoa Pudding
- Dinner: Roast Chicken, Green Beans, and Blackberries

Week 6

Monday

- Fruit: Strawberries
- Grain: Millet
- Meat: Beef
- Milk: Coconut
- Oil: Coconut
- Sweetener: Cane Sugar
- Vegetable: Asparagus

- Breakfast: Irish Soda Bread
- Snack: Macadamia Nuts
- Lunch: Roast Beef Sandwiches on Millet Bread and Strawberries
- Snack: Irish Soda Bread
- Dinner: Beef Hotdogs, Millet Mini Loafs, Asparagus, and Strawberries

Tuesday

- Fruit: Papaya
- Grain: Buckwheat
- Meat: Meat-Free Day
- Milk: Almond
- Oil: Almond
- Sweetener: Maple Syrup
- Vegetable: Zucchini

- Breakfast: Buckwheat Pancakes
- Snack: Almonds
- Lunch: Almond Butter, Buckwheat Crackers, and Papaya
- Snack: Almond Cookies
- Dinner: Buckwheat Pasta, Zucchini, and Papaya

Wednesday

- Fruit: Raspberry
- Grain: Oatmeal
- Meat: Fish
- Milk: Oatmeal
- Oil: Pecan
- Sweetener: Stevia
- Vegetable: Potato

- Breakfast: Oatmeal
- Snack: Pecans
- Lunch: Pecan Butter, Oat Bread, and Raspberry
- Snack: Oatmeal Cookies
- Dinner: Fish, French Fries, and Raspberry

Thursday

- Fruit: Grapes
- Grain: Quinoa
- Meat: Turkey
- Milk: Hemp
- Oil: Hemp
- Sweetener: Honey
- Vegetable: Broccoli

- Breakfast: Quinoa
- Snack: Cashews and Raisins
- Lunch: Quinoa Crackers, Deli Turkey, and Grapes
- Snack: Quinoa Pudding
- Dinner: Roasted Turkey Breast, Broccoli, and Grapes

Friday

- Fruit: Pears
- Grain: Sorghum
- Meat: Chicken
- Milk: Coconut
- Oil: Coconut
- Sweetener: Agave
- Vegetable: Green Beans

- Breakfast: Sorghum Muffins
- Snack: Walnuts
- Lunch: Walnut Butter, Sorghum Mini Loafs, and Pears
- Snack: Sorghum Muffins
- Dinner: Chicken Burritos on Sorghum Tortillas, Green Beans, and Pears

Saturday

- Fruit: Apples
- Grain: Buckwheat
- Meat: Lamb
- Milk: Almond
- Oil: Almond
- Sweetener: Maple Syrup
- Vegetable: Peas

- Breakfast: Buckwheat Pancakes
- Snack: Pistachio
- Lunch: Almond Butter, Buckwheat Crackers, and Apple
- Snack: Almond Cookies
- Dinner: Lamb Meatloaf, Peas, and Apple

Sunday

- Fruit: Blackberries
- Grain: Oatmeal
- Meat: Turkey
- Milk: Oatmeal
- Oil: Olive
- Sweetener: Stevia
- Vegetable: Sweet Potato

- Breakfast: Oat Granola
- Snack: Brazil Nuts
- Lunch: Oat Bread, Turkey Hotdogs, and Blackberries
- Snack: Oatmeal Cookies
- Dinner: Turkey Chili, Sweet Potato, and Blackberries

Week 7

Monday

- Fruit: Blueberries
- Grain: Quinoa
- Meat: Lamb
- Milk: Hemp
- Oil: Hemp
- Sweetener: Beet Sugar
- Vegetable: Broccoli

- Breakfast: Quinoa
- Snack: Cashew and Dried Blueberries
- Lunch: Quinoa Crackers, Hemp Butter, and Blueberries
- Snack: Quinoa Crackers
- Dinner: Lamb Meatloaf, Broccoli, and Blueberries

Tuesday

- Fruit: Strawberries
- Grain: Sorghum
- Meat: Fish
- Milk: Coconut
- Oil: Coconut
- Sweetener: Honey
- Vegetable: Sweet Potato

- Breakfast: Sorghum Coconut Muffins
- Snack: Walnuts
- Lunch: Sorghum Mini Loafs, Walnut Butter, and Strawberries
- Snack: Coconut Yogurt
- Dinner: Fish, Sweet Potato, and Strawberries

Wednesday

- Fruit: Grapes
- Grain: Buckwheat
- Meat: Meat Free Day
- Milk: Almond
- Oil: Almond
- Sweetener: Maple Syrup
- Vegetable: Zucchini

- Breakfast: Buckwheat Pancakes
- Snack: Almonds and Raisins
- Lunch: Buckwheat Crackers, Almond Butter, and Grapes
- Snack: Raisin Almond Cookie Bars
- Dinner: Buckwheat Pasta, Zucchini, and Grapes

Thursday

- Fruit: Blueberries
- Grain: Quinoa
- Meat: Lamb
- Milk: Cashew
- Oil: Cashew
- Sweetener: Beet Sugar
- Vegetable: Broccoli

- Breakfast: Quinoa
- Snack: Cashew and Dried Blueberries
- Lunch: Quinoa Crackers, Hemp Butter, and Blueberries
- Snack: Quinoa Pudding
- Dinner: Lamb Meatloaf, Broccoli, and Blueberries

Friday

- Fruit: Apples
- Grain: Rice
- Meat: Turkey
- Milk: Rice
- Oil: Olive Oil
- Sweetener: Brown Rice Syrup
- Vegetable: Peas

- Breakfast: Rice with Cinnamon and Brown Rice Syrup
- Snack: Brazil Nuts
- Lunch: Rice Crackers, Deli Turkey, and Apples
- Snack: Rice Yogurt
- Dinner: Turkey Chili, Peas, and Apples

Saturday

- Fruit: Pears
- Grain: Buckwheat
- Meat: Chicken
- Milk: Coconut
- Oil: Coconut
- Sweetener: Maple Syrup
- Vegetable: Broccoli

- Breakfast: Buckwheat Pancakes
- Snack: Pecans
- Lunch: Buckwheat Crackers, Pecan Butter, and Pears
- Snack: Coconut Milk Yogurt
- Dinner: Chicken Sausage Pizza, Broccoli, and Pears

Sunday

- Fruit: Blackberries
- Grain: Almond Meal
- Meat: Meat Free Day
- Milk: Almond
- Oil: Almond
- Sweetener: Agave
- Vegetable: Spinach

- Breakfast: Almond Meal Pancakes
- Snack: Pistachio
- Lunch: Almond Crackers, Almond Butter, and Blackberries
- Snack: Almond Cookies
- Dinner: Potato Pancakes, Spinach, and Blackberries

Week 8

Monday

- Fruit: Strawberries
- Grain: Millet
- Meat: Beef
- Milk: Coconut
- Oil: Coconut
- Sweetener: Cane Sugar
- Vegetable: Asparagus

- Breakfast: Irish Soda Bread
- Snack: Macadamia Nuts
- Lunch: Roast Beef Sandwiches on Millet Mini Loafs and Strawberries
- Snack: Coconut Milk Yogurt
- Dinner: Beef Hamburgers on Millet Mini Loaf, Asparagus, and Strawberries

Tuesday

- Fruit: Papaya
- Grain: Buckwheat
- Meat: Meat Free Day
- Milk: Hemp
- Oil: Hemp
- Sweetener: Maple Syrup
- Vegetable: Zucchini

- Breakfast: Buckwheat Pancakes
- Snack: Hemp Yogurt
- Lunch: Almond Butter, Buckwheat Crackers, and Papaya
- Snack: Hemp Pudding
- Dinner: Buckwheat Pasta, Zucchini, and Papaya

Wednesday

- Fruit: Raspberries
- Grain: Oatmeal
- Meat: Fish
- Milk: Oat
- Oil: Pecan
- Sweetener: Honey
- Vegetable: Potato

- Breakfast: Oatmeal
- Snack: Pecans
- Lunch: Pecan Butter Sandwiches on Oat Bread Mini Loafs and Raspberries
- Snack: Oatmeal Cookies
- Dinner: Fish, French Fries, and Raspberries

Thursday

- Fruit: Grapes
- Grain: Quinoa
- Meat: Turkey
- Milk: Cashew
- Oil: Cashew
- Sweetener: Agave
- Vegetable: Broccoli

- Breakfast: Quinoa
- Snack: Cashew and Raisins
- Lunch: Quinoa Crackers, Deli Turkey, and Grapes
- Snack: Quinoa Pudding
- Dinner: Roasted Turkey Breast, Broccoli, and Grapes

Friday

- Fruit: Pears
- Grain: Sorghum
- Meat: Chicken
- Milk: Coconut
- Oil: Coconut
- Sweetener: Cane Sugar
- Vegetable: Green Beans

- Breakfast: Sorghum Muffins
- Snack: Walnuts
- Lunch: Walnut Butter Sandwiches on Sorghum Mini Loafs and Pears
- Snack: Sorghum Muffins
- Dinner: Chicken Burritos on Sorghum Tortillas, Green Beans, and Pears

Saturday

- Fruit: Apples
- Grain: Buckwheat
- Meat: Lamb
- Milk: Almond
- Oil: Almond
- Sweetener: Maple Syrup
- Vegetable: Peas

- Breakfast: Buckwheat Pancakes
- Snack: Almonds and Dried Apples
- Lunch: Almond Butter, Buckwheat Crackers, and Apples
- Snack: Almond Cookies
- Dinner: Lamb Meatloaf, Peas, and Apples

Sunday

- Fruit: Blackberries
- Grain: Oat
- Meat: Turkey
- Milk: Oat
- Oil: Olive
- Sweetener: Agave
- Vegetable: Sweet Potato

- Breakfast: Oat Granola
- Snack: Brazil Nuts
- Lunch: Oat Bread Mini Loafs, Turkey Hotdogs, and Blackberries
- Snack: Oatmeal Cookies
- Dinner: Turkey Chili, Sweet Potatoes, and Blackberries

Week 9

Monday

- Fruit: Raspberries
- Grain: Amaranth
- Meat: Chicken
- Milk: Hemp
- Oil: Hemp
- Sweetener: Maple Syrup
- Vegetable: Broccoli

- Breakfast: Amaranth Pancakes
- Snack: Walnuts and Raspberries
- Lunch: Amaranth Bread, Walnut Butter, and Raspberries
- Snack: Hemp Pudding
- Dinner: Chicken Nuggets, Broccoli, and Raspberries

Tuesday

- Fruit: Blueberries
- Grain: Rice
- Meat: Beef
- Milk: Rice
- Oil: Olive
- Sweetener: Brown Rice Syrup
- Vegetable: Peas

- Breakfast: Rice with Cinnamon and Brown Rice Syrup
- Snack: Pecans
- Lunch: Rice Crackers, Pecan Butter, and Blueberries
- Snack: Rice Yogurt
- Dinner: Beef Fajitas, Peas, and Blueberries

Wednesday

- Fruit: Strawberries
- Grain: Quinoa
- Meat: Chicken
- Milk: Cashew
- Oil: Cashew
- Sweetener: Beet Sugar
- Vegetable: Green Beans

- Breakfast: Quinoa
- Snack: Cashews
- Lunch: Quinoa Crackers, Chicken Hotdogs, and Strawberries
- Snack: Quinoa Pudding
- Dinner: BBQ Chicken Sandwiches on Quinoa Bread, Green Beans, and Strawberries

Thursday

- Fruit: Pineapple
- Grain: Millet
- Meat: Turkey
- Milk: Coconut
- Oil: Coconut
- Sweetener: Stevia
- Vegetable: Potato

- Breakfast: Irish Soda Bread
- Snack: Pecans
- Lunch: Millet Bread, Deli Turkey, and Pineapple
- Snack: Coconut Yogurt
- Dinner: Turkey Sausage, Potato Hash, and Pineapple

Friday

- Fruit: Grapes
- Grain: Buckwheat
- Meat: Fish
- Milk: Almond
- Oil: Almonds
- Sweetener: Maple Syrup
- Vegetable: Sweet Potato

- Breakfast: Buckwheat Pancakes
- Snack: Almond and Raisins
- Lunch: Buckwheat Bread, Almond Butter, and Grapes
- Snack: Almond Cookies
- Dinner: Fish, Sweet Potato French Fries, and Grapes

Saturday

- Fruit: Apples
- Grain: Rice
- Meat: Pork
- Milk: Rice
- Oil: Olive
- Sweetener: Brown Rice Syrup
- Vegetable: Asparagus

- Breakfast: Rice with Cinnamon and Brown Rice Syrup
- Snack: Walnuts
- Lunch: Rice Crackers, Deli Ham, and Apples
- Snack: Rice Yogurt
- Dinner: Pork Meat Balls, Asparagus, and Apples

Sunday

- Fruit: Blackberries
- Grain: Quinoa
- Meat: Chicken
- Milk: Hemp
- Oil: Hemp
- Sweetener: Beet Sugar
- Vegetable: Broccoli

- Breakfast: Quinoa
- Snack: Macadamia Nuts
- Lunch: Quinoa Crackers, Hemp Butter, and Blackberries
- Snack: Quinoa Cookies
- Dinner: Chicken Sausage Pizza, Broccoli, and Blackberries

Week 10

Monday

- Fruit: Raspberries
- Grain: Millet
- Meat: Turkey
- Milk: Coconut
- Oil: Coconut
- Sweetener: Cane Sugar
- Vegetable: Peas

- Breakfast: Irish Soda Bread
- Snack: Brazil Nuts
- Lunch: Millet Bread, Deli Turkey, and Raspberries
- Snack: Coconut Yogurt
- Dinner: Turkey Hotdogs, Millet Bread, Raspberries, and Peas

Tuesday

- Fruit: Blueberries
- Grain: Buckwheat
- Meat: Meat-Free Day
- Milk: Cashew
- Oil: Cashew
- Sweetener: Maple Syrup
- Vegetable: Asparagus

- Breakfast: Buckwheat Pancakes
- Snack: Cashew and Dried Blueberries
- Lunch: Buckwheat Bread, Cashew Butter, and Blueberries
- Snack: Buckwheat Cashew Butter Cookies
- Dinner: Buckwheat Pasta, Blueberries, and Asparagus

Wednesday

- Fruit: Strawberries
- Grain: Rice
- Meat: Fish
- Milk: Rice
- Oil: Olive
- Sweetener: Brown Rice Syrup
- Vegetable: Potato

- Breakfast: Rice with Cinnamon and Brown Rice Syrup
- Snack: Walnuts
- Lunch: Rice Crackers, Walnut Butter, and Strawberries
- Snack: Goat Yogurt
- Dinner: Fish, French Fries, and Strawberries

Thursday

- Fruit: Pineapple
- Grain: Almond
- Meat: Pork
- Milk: Almond
- Oil: Almond
- Sweetener: Stevia
- Vegetable: Green Beans

- Breakfast: Almond Pancakes
- Snack: Macadamia Nuts
- Lunch: Almond Crackers, Deli Ham, and Pineapple
- Snack: Almond Cookies
- Dinner: Pork Chops, Green Beans, and Pineapple

Friday

- Fruit: Grapes
- Grain: Oat
- Meat: Chicken
- Milk: Hemp
- Oil: Hemp
- Sweetener: Cane Sugar
- Vegetable: Peas

- Breakfast: Oatmeal
- Snack: Brazil Nuts and Raisins
- Lunch: Oat Bread, Hemp Butter, and Grapes
- Snack: Chocolate Hemp Milk Pudding
- Dinner: Chicken Pizza, Peas, and Grapes

Saturday

- Fruit: Apples
- Grain: Buckwheat
- Meat: Beef
- Milk: Cashew
- Oil: Cashew
- Sweetener: Maple Syrup
- Vegetable: Cauliflower

- Breakfast: Buckwheat Pancakes
- Snack: Cashews
- Lunch: Buckwheat Bread, Goat Cheese, and Apples
- Snack: Cashew Yogurt
- Dinner: Meatloaf, Cauliflower, and Apples

Sunday

- Fruit: Blackberries
- Grain: Millet
- Meat: Turkey
- Milk: Coconut
- Oil: Coconut
- Sweetener: Cane Sugar
- Vegetable: Broccoli

- Breakfast: Irish Soda Bread
- Snack: Pecans
- Lunch: Millet Bread, Pecan Butter, and Blackberries
- Snack: Coconut Yogurt
- Dinner: Roasted Turkey Breast, Broccoli, and Blackberries

Week 11

Monday

- Fruit: Raspberries
- Grain: Almond
- Meat: Fish
- Milk: Almond
- Oil: Almond
- Sweetener: Stevia
- Vegetable: Potato

- Breakfast: Almond Meal Pancakes
- Snack: Macadamia Nuts
- Lunch: Almond Crackers, Almond Butter, and Raspberries
- Snack: Almond Cookies
- Dinner: Fish, French Fries, and Raspberries

Tuesday

- Fruit: Blueberries
- Grain: Oat
- Meat: Chicken
- Milk: Hemp
- Oil: Hemp
- Sweetener: Honey
- Vegetable: Asparagus

- Breakfast: Oatmeal

- Snack: Cashew and Dried Blueberries

- Lunch: Oat Bread, Deli Chicken, and Blueberries

- Snack: Hemp Milk Pudding

- Dinner: Chicken Burritos, Blueberry, and Asparagus

Wednesday

- Fruit: Strawberries

- Grain: Buckwheat

- Meat: Meat Free Day

- Milk: Cashew

- Oil: Cashew

- Sweetener: Maple Syrup

- Vegetable: Green Beans

- Breakfast: Buckwheat Pancakes

- Snack: Pecans

- Lunch: Buckwheat Bread, Goat Cheese, and Strawberries

- Snack: Cashew Yogurt

- Dinner: Buckwheat Pasta, Strawberries, and Green Beans

Thursday

- Fruit: Pineapple
- Grain: Millet
- Meat: Turkey
- Milk: Coconut
- Oil: Coconut
- Sweetener: Cane Sugar
- Vegetable: Peas

- Breakfast: Irish Soda Bread
- Snack: Walnuts
- Lunch: Millet Bread, Deli Turkey, and Pineapple
- Snack: Coconut Milk Yogurt
- Dinner: Roasted Turkey, Pineapple, and Peas

Friday

- Fruit: Grapes
- Grain: Almond Meal
- Meat: Beef
- Milk: Almond
- Oil: Almond
- Sweetener: Maple Syrup
- Vegetable: Broccoli

- Breakfast: Almond Pancakes
- Snack: Brazil Nuts and Raisins
- Lunch: Almond Crackers, Almond Butter, and Grapes
- Snack: Almond Cookies
- Dinner: Hamburger Patty (No Bun), Broccoli, and Grapes

Saturday

- Fruit: Apples
- Grain: Sorghum
- Meat: Chicken
- Milk: Hemp
- Oil: Hemp
- Sweetener: Beet Sugar
- Vegetable: Green Beans

- Breakfast: Sorghum Muffins
- Snack: Macadamia Nuts
- Lunch: Sorghum Bread, Hemp Butter, and Apples
- Snack: Applesauce
- Dinner: Pizza with Chicken Sausage, Green Beans, and Apples

Sunday

- Fruit: Blackberries
- Grain: Buckwheat
- Meat: Meat Free Day
- Milk: Cashew
- Oil: Cashew
- Sweetener: Maple Syrup
- Vegetable: Salad Greens

- Breakfast: Buckwheat Pancakes
- Snack: Cashews
- Lunch: Buckwheat Bread, Cashew Butter, and Blackberries
- Snack: Cashew Yogurt
- Dinner: Buckwheat Pasta, Blackberries, and Salad

Week 12

Monday

- Fruit: Blueberries
- Grain: Oat
- Meat: Chicken
- Milk: Hemp
- Oil: Hemp
- Sweetener: Honey
- Vegetable: Asparagus

- Breakfast:
- Snack:
- Lunch:
- Snack:
- Dinner:

Tuesday

- Fruit: Strawberries
- Grain: Buckwheat
- Meat: Meat Free Day
- Milk: Cashew
- Oil: Cashew
- Sweetener: Maple Syrup
- Vegetable: Green Beans
- Breakfast:
- Snack:
- Lunch:
- Snack:
- Dinner:

Wednesday

- Fruit: Pineapple
- Grain: Millet
- Meat: Turkey
- Milk: Coconut
- Oil: Coconut
- Sweetener: Coconut Sugar
- Vegetable: Peas
- Breakfast:
- Snack:
- Lunch:
- Snack:
- Dinner:

Thursday

- Fruit: Grapes
- Grain: Almond Meal
- Meat: Beef
- Milk: Almond
- Oil: Almond
- Sweetener: Maple Syrup
- Vegetable: Broccoli
- Breakfast:
- Snack:
- Lunch:
- Snack:
- Dinner:

Friday

- Fruit: Apples
- Grain: Sorghum
- Meat: Chicken
- Milk: Hemp
- Oil: Hemp
- Sweetener: Beet Sugar
- Vegetable: Green Beans
- Breakfast:
- Snack:
- Lunch:
- Snack:
- Dinner:

Saturday

- Fruit: Blackberries
- Grain: Buckwheat
- Meat: Meat Free Day
- Milk: Cashew
- Oil: Cashew
- Sweetener: Maple Syrup
- Vegetable: Salad Green
- Breakfast:
- Snack:
- Lunch:
- Snack:
- Dinner:

Sunday

- Fruit: Pineapple
- Grain: Almond
- Meat: Pork
- Milk: Almond
- Oil: Almond
- Sweetener: Stevia
- Vegetable: Green Beans
- Breakfast:
- Snack:
- Lunch:
- Snack:
- Dinner:
- Breakfast

Breakfast

Mornings can be rough when you have children. Not only do you have to get yourself up and ready, which is never easy, but now you are expected to help motivate other people to do something that, and let's be real here, you really don't want to do yourself. We all want to stay in our PJs for a few more minutes if not hours and add to that multiple food allergies or a rotation diet and feeding said unmotivated people becomes a task that could easily send the strongest of parents under the bed for cover; which is why you won't find recipes here that call for actual work. Each recipe has a simple ingredient list, and all are approved by my own Funky Food kids.

Buckwheat Pancakes

These are one of my family's favorites and frankly I like them better than the wheat version. (Confession time: sometimes my wheat pancakes are gummy in the middle because I get bored and don't want to cook them long enough.) I never have that problem with these. They rise beautifully, and buckwheat doesn't get all crumbly like some of the other allergen-free grains, so you don't have to add a binding agent like xanthan gum. This one is perfect for buckwheat day in a rotation diet!

Ingredients:

- 1 c. Buckwheat Flour (I prefer to mill my own; it has a better texture)
- 1 tsp. Baking Soda
- 1 tsp. Cream of Tartar
- 1/2 tsp. Salt
- 1 c. Rice Milk
- 3 Tbsp. Canola Oil

Preheat nonstick skillet. Whisk together the dry ingredients. Add in the remaining ingredients and stir until combined. Pour spoonfuls onto the skillet and cook until the tops start to bubble and the edges brown. Flip and cook until lightly brown. Top with maple syrup, honey, or agave nectar.

Funky Options:

- Add in any of the following—1/2 cup Chopped Pecans, 1/4 cup Hulled Hemp Seeds, 2 tablespoons Cinnamon, 1/2 teaspoon Nutmeg

- Milk Alternatives—use any milk that your child can tolerate, apple juice, or even water!

- Flour Alternatives—3/4 cup flour of choice (Rice, Teff, Oat, etc.) and 1/4 cup starch of choice (Arrowroot, Tapioca, etc.)

Amaranth Pancakes

Amaranth was one of the first grains I fell in love with after Landon was diagnosed with EG. Like most toddlers, he wasn't a huge fan of meat and with his limited diet I was concerned about him getting enough balanced proteins. Amaranth is one of the few non-meat sources of essential amino acids, so I started using it in just about everything. This was one of my first Funky Food recipes, Enjoy!

Ingredients:

- 1 c. Amaranth Flour
- 1/2 c. Tapioca Starch
- 1 tsp. Baking Soda
- 1 tsp. Cream of Tartar
- 1/2 tsp. Salt
- 1 1/2 c. Hemp Milk
- 2 Tbsp. Canola Oil

Preheat nonstick skillet. Whisk together the dry ingredients. Add in the remaining ingredients and stir until combined. Pour spoonfuls onto the skillet and cook until the tops start to bubble and the edges brown. Flip and cook until lightly brown. Top with maple syrup, honey, or agave nectar.

Funky Options:

- Add any of the following: 1/2 cup chopped Walnuts, 1/4 cup Flaxseed Meal, 2 teaspoons Cinnamon, 3 tablespoons Maple Syrup

- Flour Substitutions: 1 cup Buckwheat, Sorghum, or Millet, and 1/2 c. Arrowroot or Potato Starch

- Milk Substitutions: 1 1/2 cup Coconut, Rice, or Pumpkin Seed Milk

Carob Muffins

There is something about serving children chocolate (carob) muffins that makes me feel like I've gotten away with something. Please imagine me rubbing my hands together while quietly cackling with glee at the fast one I just pulled over my unsuspecting children. These muffins seem like a treat but are packed full of nutrients!

Ingredients:

- 1 c. Amaranth Flour
- 1/2 c. Teff Flour
- 1/2 c. Carob or Cocoa Powder
- 1/3 c. Sugar
- 2 tsp. Cream of Tartar
- 2 1/4 tsp. Baking Soda
- 1/2 tsp. Salt
- 1/2 c. Applesauce
- 3 Tbsp. Canola Oil
- 1 Tbsp. Vanilla
- 1 c. Rice Milk Yogurt or Rice Milk

Preheat oven to 400 degrees and grease muffin tin. Mix together dry ingredients. Then add in wet ingredients and stir until moist, but don't over mix. Spoon into muffin tin—makes 12 large muffins. Bake for about 12 minutes.

Funky Options:

- Add in any of the following: 1/2 cup chopped Pecans, 1/4 cup Dairy-Free Chocolate Chips, or 1/2 cup Flaxseed Meal

- Applesauce Substitution: 1/2 cup any fruit/veggie puree (Squash, Pumpkin, Sweet Potato, or Pear)

- Milk/Yogurt Substitutions: Coconut. Sunflower Seed, or Hemp

Coconut Sorghum Muffins

I love cooking with coconut milk and flour. It adds just the right amount of "something" to a muffin, making it moist and delicious. I added some molasses to this recipe for extra calcium. Molasses is a great way to get calcium into a dairy-free diet!

Ingredients:

- 1 1/4 c. Sorghum Flour
- 1/2 c. Tapioca Starch
- 1/4 c. Coconut Flour
- 1/2 c. Sugar
- 2 tsp. Cream of Tartar
- 2 tsp. Baking Soda
- 1/4 c. Applesauce
- 3 Tbsp. Canola Oil
- 1 tsp. Vanilla
- 1 Tbsp. Molasses
- 1 1/4 c. Coconut Milk
- Shredded Coconut for topping

Preheat oven to 400 degrees and grease muffin tin. Mix together dry ingredients. Add remaining ingredients, combine, and stir gently until moistened. Don't over mix. Spoon batter into muffin cups and sprinkle with shredded coconut. Bake for 10-12 minutes.

Funky Options:

- Add in any of the following: 1/2 cup chopped Almonds, 1/4 cup Hulled Hemp Seeds, 1/2 teaspoon ginger, or 1/2 cup Vegan Chocolate Chips

- Applesauce Substitutions: 1/4 cup of any fruit/veggie puree

Gingerbread Muffins

Muffins are an allergen-free cooking must. They are easy to make, quick to bake, and with a good variety, they are a breakfast staple that no one will get tired of. This recipe is one I love to make in the winter as it makes my house smell delicious!

Ingredients:

- 1 c. Amaranth Flour
- 1 c. Sorghum Flour
- 1/3 c. Sugar
- 2 tsp. Cream of Tartar
- 2 1/4 tsp. Baking Soda
- 1/2 tsp. Salt
- 1 tsp. Cinnamon
- 1/2 tsp. Ginger
- 1/4 tsp. Cloves
- 1/2 c. Applesauce
- 1 Tbsp. Molasses
- 3 Tbsp. Canola Oil
- 1 tsp. Vanilla
- 1 c. Milk or Yogurt of choice
- Turbinado Sugar for topping

Preheat oven to 400 degrees and grease muffin tin. Mix together dry ingredients. Add remaining ingredients, combine, and stir gently until moistened. Don't over mix. Spoon batter into muffin cups and sprinkle with turbinado sugar. Bake for 10-12 minutes.

Tip: The turbinado sugar adds a great crunch and touch of sweetness to these muffins, but only use it if you are planning on serving immediately. The sugar will get gooey if you store over-night.

Funky Options:

- Add in any of the following: 1/4 cup Hulled Hemp Seeds, 1/2 cup chopped Pecans, 1/2 cup Raisins

- Applesauce Substitutions: 1/2 cup of any of the following: Butternut Squash, Pumpkin, Banana, Squash, Zucchini, or Pear

Crockpot Granola

Granola is gloriously versatile but that can also be its downfall when trying to buy in the store. It's packed with so many different ingredients it can be all but impossible to find one that fits a Funky Food diet. And don't get me started on how much sugar and fat that can hide in this "health food" staple. This recipe gives you the best of both worlds: a granola that you can tailor to fit your allergen needs without all the sugar and fat! Stacy over at A Year of Slow Cooking Blog inspired this recipe with her Crockpot cooking genius—check her out!

Ingredients:

- 5 c. Gluten-free Oatmeal or Quinoa Flakes
- 1/4 c. Applesauce
- 1/4 c. Honey
- 3 Tbsp. Molasses (omit if needed)
- Several teaspoons of any or all of the following:
- Cinnamon
- Ginger
- Nutmeg
- Vanilla

Pour applesauce, honey, and molasses into a 4-quart Crockpot, and stir to combine. Toss remaining ingredients into a large Crockpot and stir till combined. Vent lid with a wooden spoon.

Cook on high for 3-4 hours but stir every 20-30 minutes. About halfway through the cooking process is when you should throw in any coconut, nuts, or seeds. I've had a batch burn the nuts long before the oats were toasted so I put mine in after a couple hours of cooking. Once oats are a gorgeous brown, pour granola onto a baking sheet to cool. Store in an airtight container.

Funky Options:

- Add in any of the following: 1 cup chopped Pecans, Almonds, Hazelnuts, Walnuts; 1/2 cup dried fruit (after cooled), and 1/2 cup shredded Coconut

- Applesauce Substitutions: Use 1/4 cup any of the following fruit/veggie purees: Pear, Butternut Squash, Pumpkin, Squash, or Banana

- Honey Substitutions: 1/4 cup of any of the following: Agave Nectar, Brown Rice Syrup, Simple Cane Sugar Syrup, Golden Syrup, or Maple Syrup

Irish Soda Bread

Known as "breakfast cake" to the Swindle kids, this soda bread is moist and delicious. It is the perfect way to start a Saturday morning or entice a reluctant child out of a warm bed. Katrina over at the Gluten-Free Goddess helped inspire this recipe—she is a must for anyone trying to bake gluten-free!

Ingredients:

- 1 1/2 c. Millet
- 1/2 c. Tapioca Starch
- 1 3/4 tsp. Baking Soda
- 3/4 tsp. Cream of Tartar
- 2 Tbsp. Sugar
- 1 tsp. Salt
- 2 tsp. Xanthan Gum

Mix together and form a well to pour in:

- 3/4 c. Coconut Milk
- 1 tsp. Apple Cider Vinegar
- 1/2 c. Applesauce
- 5 Tbsp. Canola oil
- 2 Tbsp. Honey

Preheat oven to 350 and grease 8-inch cake pan. Stir wet ingredients into dry until they form a smooth cake-like batter. Pour into cake pan and spread flat. Cut an 'X' into the top of the batter—this is important as it will bring you good luck. Bake for 30-45 minutes or until golden brown. Do not under-bake or the xanthan gum will turn this recipe into goo. Not that I've ever done that, more than once.

Funky Options:

- Add in any of the following: 1/2 cup Dairy-free Chocolate Chips, 1/4 cup Hemp Seeds, 1/2 cup chopped Pecans or 1/2 dried Cranberries

- Flour Substitutions: 1 1/2 cups Sorghum or 1 cup Rice and 1/2 cup Tapioca Starch

Strawberry Rhubarb Muffins

Wait! Before you flip on by, let me sell you on these muffins. Rhubarb looks like celery that has spent an afternoon with a 3-year-old girl and her crayon box. It's a gorgeous shade of pinky red. It's packed with Vitamin C and the super sweetness of the strawberries balance the flavor of the rhubarb perfectly. They give these muffins just the right, well, something. You can find them in the freezer section already chopped or look at your local farmer's market in March and April.

Ingredients:

- 1 1/2 c. Sorghum Flour
- 1/2 c. Tapioca Starch
- 1/2 c. Sugar
- 2 tsp. Cream of Tartar
- 2 tsp. Baking Soda
- 1/4 c. Applesauce
- 3 Tbsp. Canola Oil
- 1 tsp. Vanilla
- 1 1/2 c. Milk or Yogurt
- 1/4 c. Chopped Rhubarb
- 1/4 c. Chopped Strawberries
- Turbinado Sugar for topping

Preheat oven to 400 degrees and grease muffin tin. Mix together dry ingredients. Add remaining ingredients, combine, and stir gently until moistened. Don't over mix. Spoon batter into muffin cups and sprinkle with turbinado sugar. Bake for 10-12 minutes.

Tip: If you are going to store these, don't top with the turbindo sugar—it gets gooey!

Funky Options:

- Add in any of the following: 1/4 cup Hulled Hemp Seeds, 1/2 cup chopped Pecans, or 1/2 cup chopped Macadamia Nuts

- Applesauce Substitutions: 1/4 cup Strawberry Yogurt or pureed Strawberries

Bread

This is the holy grail of allergen baking. Our food lives are centered around bread and grains. Pasta, sandwiches, crackers, tortillas, pizza, or a gorgeous baguette, it's an important staple in our food culture. Trying to live without it is nearly impossible and can be downright miserable to a child. Landon was about two years old when he had his very first sunflower seed butter and jelly sandwich that looked just like his big brother's PB&J. I didn't realize how much he was feeling left out until I handed him that sandwich. His whole face lit up and he proclaimed "I eat just like Brenden!" Here are several of my favorite breads that you can make to help your family eat just like everyone else too.

Tortillas

Tortillas are great for anyone living with food allergies or on a rotation diet. Almost any grain will work and the ingredients list is short, so you can make it fit your individual needs. These make fantastic quesadillas, or rolled up with your favorite nut butter or sliced turkey!

Ingredients:

- 1/2 c Amaranth Flour
- 1/2 tsp. Salt
- 1 Tbsp. Extra Virgin Olive Oil
- Enough water to make a thick dough—less water is better. You can always add more.

Heat some oil in a skillet. Combine dry ingredients, stir in extra virgin olive oil, and then add a little water at a time until your flour forms into a ball. It will be pretty sticky. Heavily flour a cutting board or countertop with amaranth flour. Form a ball about 3 inches across. Place it onto the floured surface. Gently begin to pat the dough ball with floured fingertips until you form a very thin, round tortilla. It will be very fragile. Using a spatula gently pick it up and place into a heated and oiled skillet. Let it cook for a couple of minutes on both sides.

Funky Options:

- Add any of the following: 4 tablespoons Hemp Seeds, 2 teaspoons Oregano, or 2 teaspoons Lime Juice

- Flour Substitutions: Any you can think of! Millet, Rice, Sorghum, Teff, Oat, etc.

Breadcrumbs

You need breadcrumbs! This is one of those ingredients I didn't give much thought to after Landon's diagnosis until one evening I went to go make a meatloaf and was faced with the realization that I had nothing in the house that would work. Thankfully, this is a simple problem to remedy!

Ingredients:

- 5 slices of your homemade bread

Preheat oven to 200 degrees. Place bread slices on a baking sheet. Bake forever or at least until very, very dry. Let cool. Then run through your food processor or place in a plastic bag and beat till you make crumbs.

Funky Options:

No time? Try using certified gluten-free oatmeal or quinoa flakes in place of breadcrumbs. Both work great!

Bread Machine Bread

Landon loves bread, as only someone who can't have it all the time can. This recipe uses spelt, it does contain gluten but is sometimes tolerated well by people with "food intolerance" like Landon. I have included several great substitutions for the spelt below the recipe for anyone going gluten-free! I use the Breadman Bread Machine's gluten-free cycle. It only has one rise, so it seems to make loftier gluten-free bread.

Ingredients:

- 1 1/4 c. Hot Water
- 3 Tbsp. Extra Virgin Olive Oil
- 2 tsp. Salt
- 4 tsp. Honey
- 3 Tbsp. Powdered Rice Milk
- 3 c. Spelt
- 1 c. Amaranth
- 1 Tbsp. Yeast

Set machine for 2-pound loaf, medium color, and use either gluten-free cycle or whole wheat cycle. If you don't have a gluten-free cycle I really recommend only using one rise and baking it in your oven instead. Wet stuff goes in first, then salt, then flours, and finally the yeast. Keep the salt and yeast away from each other.

Funky Options:

- 2 c. Rice Flour
- 1 c. Amaranth Flour
- 1 c. Tapioca Starch

Or

- 2 c. Buckwheat Flour
- 1 c. Amaranth Flour
- 1 c. Tapioca Starch

Crackers

I love these crackers. Landon loves these crackers. They are easy to make, a cinch to fit into his rotation diet, and taste fantastic. Don't be intimidated by making your own crackers. After the first time you make them, you may never want store-bought crackers again! I am not the biggest fan of quinoa flour; it has such a strong flavor that I find it overwhelming in breads. But in this recipe it tastes great giving the crackers a nutty flavor. If you are craving a graham type cracker flavor, try using sweet sorghum flour—yum!

Ingredients:

- 1 c. Quinoa Flour
- 1/4 c. Tapioca Starch
- 1/2 tsp. Salt
- 1 tsp. Apple Cider Vinegar
- 2 tsp. Extra Virgin Olive Oil
- 4-6 Tbsp. Warm Water

Preheat oven to 400 degrees. Mix flours well with salt. Add apple cider vinegar and oil. Mix until coarse mixture forms. Add water until dough comes together. Knead the dough until even textured and forms a ball, not sticky. Place half on parchment paper, flatten, and cover with second piece of parchment paper. Roll out until paper thin. Peel away top piece of parchment paper and slice into whatever shape floats your cracker-eating fancy. Place on a Silpat or silicone-lined baking sheet and bake for roughly 15 minutes.

Funky Options:

- Add in any of the following: 1/4 cup Hemp Seeds, 1/4 cup Finely Diced Pecans, or top with a sprinkle of Sea Salt

- Flour Substitutions: Millet, Sorghum, Amaranth, Teff, Buckwheat, or Almond Meal

Faux "Corn" Bread

As anyone who is allergic to corn knows, corn is in everything! For the most part it's used as a sugar, so it's easy to replace in a homemade version. But in cornbread, you have to get a little creative to find the perfect substitution. I love using amaranth in this recipe because it has a fine grit to it, similar to cornmeal.

Ingredients:

- 1 c. Amaranth
- 1/2 c. Tapioca Starch
- 1 1/2 tsp. Cream of Tartar
- 1 1/2 tsp. Baking Soda
- 2/3 c. Water or Milk of Choice
- 1/4 c. Honey, Maple Syrup, or Agave Nectar
- 3 Tbsp. Extra Virgin Olive Oil

Preheat oven to 375 degrees and oil a 9-inch pie plate or 8x8-inch baking dish. Mix together your dry ingredients. Stir in all the remaining ingredients until combined. Pour into the prepared pan and smooth. Bake for 18-20 minutes or until a toothpick comes out clean. Cool for about 10 minutes before serving.

Funky Options:

Add in one or two of the following: 1 cup Shredded Cheese, Diced Green Chiles, 2-3 tablespoons Sugar, 1/2 cup minced Pine Nuts
Flour Substitutions: Buckwheat or Millet

Hamburger Buns

One of my regular readers on my blog asked if I had ever made hamburger buns. Well, I hadn't, so I thought I would give it a try. I found the original version of this recipe on another of my favorite blogs, Gaggle of Girls, so I made it work for my own Funky Food kid and we loved it! You can also pour this straight into your bread machine and make a gorgeous loaf of bread. I like using millet for this recipe as it gives the hamburger buns a lovely color and texture.

Ingredients:

- 1 c. Water
- 2 Tbsp. Extra Virgin Olive Oil
- 1/2 c. Applesauce
- 2 tsp. Apple Cider Vinegar
- 1 3/4 c. Millet Flour
- 1 c. Tapioca Starch
- 2 1/2 tsp. Xanthan Gum
- 1 1/4 tsp. Salt
- 2 Tbsp. Sugar
- 2 tsp. Yeast

I used the dough cycle on my bread machine, but you can use a stand mixer with the dough hook to make this dough. It will be very wet—more like a muffin/cake batter than bread dough so don't try to do this by hand. It won't work, but a stand mixer will. Combine wet ingredients first, then dry, and top with yeast. Once your dough is made, preheat your oven to 350 degrees. I made hamburger bun molds out of circles of aluminum foil but you can use English Muffin molds or I found hamburger bun pans and hotdogs pans online. Using a spoon drop several teaspoonfuls of the dough into each mold placed on a greased baking sheet. Bake for about 10-12 minutes or until golden brown. Let cool slightly before slicing.

Funky Options:

- Add in any of the following: 1/4 cup Hemp Seeds, 3 teaspoons diced Red Onion, or 2 teaspoons Italian Herbs

Pizza Dough

Living with multiple food allergies can be rough on a kid. Expecting them to live without pizza isn't fair, so I patched together a recipe that I can make in my bread machine that makes great pizza dough. I have used spelt in this recipe to help give the dough a little help, but you'll find plenty of alternatives below. Remember to avoid spelt if you have an allergy to gluten!

Ingredients:

- 1 1/4 c. Water
- 2 Tbsp. Extra Virgin Olive Oil
- 2 c. Spelt
- 1 1/4 c. Amaranth
- 1 tsp. Sugar
- 1 Tbsp. Yeast

Use the dough cycle on your bread machine. Place wet ingredients in first, then add in the dry, and top with the yeast. After dough is finished, preheat the oven to 450 degrees. Roll out dough into desired thickness. Place onto pizza stone or oiled baking sheet. Use a fork to prick a bazillion little holes on the pizza crust—this will keep your crust from bubbling. and bake for 8 minutes or until golden. Pull out of oven and top with favorite toppings and cheese. Put back into oven for another 10-15 minutes or until cheese is melted. Let cool for a couple minutes before cutting.

Funky Options:

- Add in any of the following: 1/4 cup parmesan cheese, 3 tablespoons Italian Herbs, or 1 tablespoon cinnamon for a dessert pizza

- Flour Substitution: 1 cup Rice Flour, 1 cup Buckwheat Flour, 1 cup Amaranth Flour, 1/4 cup Tapioca Starch

Yeast-Free Pizza Dough

Sometimes you forget to start your yeast pizza dough, or completely forget to add the yeast to the bread machine. Thankfully, you have a Plan B, and this recipe is it! This is also a great recipe for anyone avoiding yeast in their diet. Enjoy!

Ingredients:

- 3/4 c. Millet
- 1/4 c. Tapioca Starch
- 2 tsp. Cream of Tartar
- 2 tsp. Baking Soda
- 2 tsp. Apple Cider Vinegar
- ¼ tsp. Xantham Gum
- 4 Tbsp. Extra Virgin Olive Oil
- 1 1/2 tsp. Salt
- 1/4 c. Water

Preheat oven to 400 degrees and grease baking sheet. Mix dry ingredients together and add everything but the water. Stir in the water. You are looking for moist dough that easily forms a ball when kneaded. Add a little extra water if needed. Press onto baking sheet into whatever thickness desired. Before adding toppings bake for about 5 minutes. Then pull out and put your favorite toppings on, slide it back into the oven, and enjoy when crust is slightly brown and toppings are bubbling.

Funky Options:

- Add in any of the following: 1/4 cup Parmesan Cheese, 3 tablespoons Italian Herbs, or 1 tablespoon Cinnamon for a dessert pizza

- Flour Substitutions: Buckwheat, Sorghum, Amaranth, Teff, or Oat

Meals

For the most part, lunch and dinner were the simplest recipes to fit Landon's dietary needs, hence this chapter's length compared to the others. I wasn't going to complain about an easy step in learning how to feed a family Funky Food!

Butternut Squash Pasta

Living without dairy does not mean giving up creamy sauces for your pasta. This one is rich, creamy, and my boys love it!

Ingredients:

- 1 c. Butternut Squash Puree
- 1 c. Coconut Milk
- 3 Cloves Garlic Diced
- 1/8 c. Fresh Sage Chopped (or 2 tsp dried)
- 1/4 lb. Sausage Cooked
- Serve over Rice Pasta

Start your pasta water, and don't forget to add the pasta when it boils (not that I have ever done that). In a skillet, sauté garlic and sage in a little extra virgin olive oil. When it starts to smell divine, pour in the butternut squash puree and combine. Whisk in the rice milk until smooth and creamy. Add salt and pepper for taste. As this cooks, it will condense a lot. I ended up whisking in 2 cups of the hot pasta water. Add in the sausage for the final step. Serve over rice pasta.

Funky Options:

- Substitutions for the Butternut Squash: Sweet Potato or any other Yellow Squash puree
- Substitutions for Coconut Milk: Almond Milk or Hemp Milk

Chicken Nuggets

I love using millet flour in this recipe because it gives the nuggets that all-important yellow color, especially if you have children. The boys think these look and taste exactly the "real" deal so feel free to taste test your clan!

Ingredients:

- 1 lb. Chicken Breasts, cubed
- 1 c. Almond Milk
- 1 c. Millet Flour
- 3 tsp. Spice of Choice (Italian spices, Paprika, or Salt and Pepper)

Preheat oven to 425 degrees. Coat chicken with almond milk. To contain the mess, you can put the millet flour in a Ziploc bag along with the spices. Put a handful of chicken in at a time and practice your best "Shake and Bake" imitation. Spread coated chicken nuggets on a greased baking sheet in a single layer. Bake for 8 minutes, then flip over, and bake for another 8 minutes.

Funky Options:

- Chicken Substitutions: Turkey, Lamb, Beef, or Pork
- Almond Milk Substitutions: Any other milk
- Millet Flour Substitutions: Buckwheat, Amaranth, or Oat

Chicken Salad

This recipe goes wonderfully with the cracker or tortilla recipes included in this book. This would make a great school lunch or dinner on a hot summer day.

Ingredients:

- 2 c. Diced Chicken
- 1 c. Coconut Milk Yogurt
- 2 tsp. Apple Cider Vinegar
- 4 tsp. Honey

Mix together everything but chicken until smooth. Pour over diced chicken. Serve chilled alone, on tortillas, or bread. A perfect meal for a sunny day.

Funky Options:

- Add any of the following: 1/2 cup Diced Pear or Apple, 1/2 cup chopped Pecans, 1/2 cup chopped Celery, or 2 teaspoons Poppy seeds

Oven Fries

These are about to be your new best friend. You can make any root vegetable into an oven fry. They are easy to prepare and cook, with the added bonus of being one of the most kid-friendly foods on the planet!

Ingredients:

- 4 Root Vegetables (See Funky Options for suggestions)
- 3 Tbsp. Extra Virgin Olive Oil
- Salt and Pepper

Preheat oven to 400 degrees. Scrub veggies. Peel the veggies if conventional or leave peels on for extra nutrients if they are organic. Cut into whatever shape tickles your fancy, remember thinner will cook faster. Toss with the olive oil. Sprinkle with at least salt and pepper or get fancy and throw on some paprika, chili powder, or cinnamon. Spread out on greased baking sheet or Silpat-lined baking sheet. Bake until at least fork tender or until they are as crispy as you like 'em about 15 minutes depending on thickness. Serve hot with your favorite dipping sauce.

Funky Options:

- Root Veggies—Turnips, Sweet Potato, Russet Potato, Rutabaga, or Celeriac

Meatloaf/Meatballs

What is not to love about meatloaf or meatballs? They are a great way to get protein into our kiddos and even some extra veggies if you're feeling sneaky!

Ingredients:

- 1 lb. Ground Turkey
- 3/4 c. Teff Bread Crumbs
- 4 Tbsp. Italian Spices
- 1/2 tsp. Salt
- 2 Tbsp. Canola Oil

Preheat oven to 400 degrees. Mix ingredients. Roll out meatballs to about 1 inch in diameter. Place on oiled baking sheet. Bake for 15 minutes or until done. To make the meatloaf simply press the meat mixture into a bread pan or baking sheet and bake for about an hour.

Funky Options:

- Turkey Substitutions: Lamb, Beef, Chicken, or Pork
- Bread Crumb Substitutions: Quinoa Flakes or any Breadcrumbs
- Add any of the following: 1/2 cup Ketchup, 1/4 cup Sweet Potato, Spinach Puree, or 1/4 cup Hemp Seeds

Snacks

Every mother knows it's all about the snacks. Whether you are on the go or have a house filled with toddlers, snacks are a must. This isn't the meal I would have thought would be the hardest hit by Landon's food allergies, but it was. Almost every snack I gave my children prior to food allergies was made by someone else. They were healthy snacks—granola bars, crackers, dried fruit, etc. yet they all contained something he couldn't eat. For the most part the cookbooks I found about food allergies focused on meals and breads. Not exactly the best things to throw in a diaper bag while running out the door for a sanity saving play date! These are some of my very first recipes I patched together. I hope they help you as much as they helped me!

Cereal Bars

A billion years and three kids ago, I was a freshman in the dorms at Oklahoma State University. I loved living in the dorms; my friends were nearby, I didn't have to clean the bathroom, and food was prepared for me everyday right downstairs. Frankly, it was an awful lot like being a kid with fewer rules. I miss it. In the cafeteria a table laden with all sorts of delectable goodies awaited my attention each evening at dinner. This is where I was first introduced to these crunchy, chewy treats. These were one of my favorite desserts and now that I have a family eating Funky Food, these fit perfectly. I can mix and match ingredients to fit easily!

Ingredients:

- 1 c. Almond Butter
- 1 c. Honey
- 1 c. Sugar
- 6 c. Oat O-Shaped Cereal (or whatever works for you!)

In a saucepan over medium heat, stir together the honey and sugar. Bring to a boil until the sugar is dissolved. Take the pan off the heat and stir in the almond butter. Then pour mixture over the cereal in a large bowl, stirring to coat. Pour the mixture into a greased 9x10 baking dish. Mush out into the dish. Let cool, cut into bars, and enjoy.

Funky Options:

- Add any of the following: 1/4 cup Hemp Seeds, 1/2 cup Chopped Nuts, or 1/4 cup Flaxseed Meal

- Almond Butter Substitutions: 1 cup Sunbutter, or Pecan Butter

- Honey Substitutions: 1 cup Maple Syrup, Brown Rice Syrup, or 1 cup Corn-Free Syrup

Granola Bars

I love these so much it borders on the ridiculous. When Landon was first diagnosed, granola bars were one of the foods that I couldn't find in the store to fit his needs. The recipes I found to make them weren't quite right either. The ingredient lists were too varied or the steps too long or they just didn't taste right. This recipe is so easy and quick, I make them every week. The boys eat them for snacks, naturally, but can be found eating them for breakfast as well. The ingredients are interchangeable, which makes it a snap to tailor them to fit any diet!

Ingredients:

- 1 c. Sunbutter
- 1 c. Honey
- 4 c. Oatmeal

Preheat the oven to 350 degrees. Mix together Sunbutter and honey until smooth. Stir in any additions before adding the oatmeal (trust me on this one). Add in oatmeal. Press onto Silpat lined or greased baking sheet about 1/2 inch thick. Bake for 15-18 minutes until golden brown. Let cool and cut into desired shape. Store in an airtight container.

Funky Options:

- Add any of the following: 1/4 cup Dairy-Free Chocolate Chips, 1/4 cup Hemp Seeds, 1/2 cup Chopped Nuts, 1/2 cup Dried Fruit

- Sunbutter Substitutions: 1 cup Hemp Butter, or 1 cup Almond Butter

- Honey Substitutions: 1 cup Maple Syrup or 1 cup Corn-Free Syrup (page 199)

- Oatmeal Substitutions: Quinoa Flakes, Puffed Millet, Puffed Amaranth, or any Cereal that fits your kiddo's needs.

Super Smoothie

This recipe not only deserves its own theme music but also a cape. This was my very first Funky Food recipe long before there was a Funky Food blog. I started making Landon smoothies to help him gain weight, reduce the inflammation in his system, and help soothe his stomach. The ingredients I chose varied as to what he was tolerating or what symptoms I was trying to help. The only core ingredient that never changed was the papaya. They are loaded with fantastic nutrients and give smoothies this wonderfully silky texture and mild sweetness.

Ingredients:

- 1 c. Rice Milk

- 1 c. Fresh Papaya

- 1/4 tsp. Children's DHA (make sure it's molecularly distilled to remove mercury)

- 1/4 tsp. Infant's Probiotics (Jarrow Formula's has an allergen free version)

- 3-4 Tbsp. Flaxseed Oil

Blend thoroughly. I have used a Bullet Blender, which I found simpler for daily use instead of a full-size blender. Place in an insulated cup with a straw. Landon was encouraged to sip at his throughout the day. I never had any problem with him not eating at mealtimes and I truly believe these smoothies helped heal his stomach and keep his weight steady.

Funky Options:

- Rice Milk Substitutions: Hemp, Almond, Oat, Pumpkin Seed, Sunflower Seed, or Coconut Milk

- Flaxseed Oil Substitutions: Extra Virgin Olive Oil, Sunflower Seed Oil, Canola Oil or Hemp Oil

Roasted Nuts

I made batches of these for years during the holidays. They make perfect gifts for teachers and friends. It was a teacher of Landon's that inspired me to find a way to make them without eggs—Thank you, Cheryl!

Ingredients:

- 1/2 c. water
- 1 Tbsp Flaxseed Meal
- 4 c. Nuts/Seeds
- 1/2 c. Sugar
- 1/4 tsp Salt
- 1/2 tsp Cinnamon

Combine the 1/2 cup water and flax meal, in a saucepan on your stovetop. Bring it to a boil. Then reduce the heat to low and cook it for about 5 minutes or until this mixture starts to look like an egg white. (It's like magic, really.)

Preheat your oven to 250 degrees. Lightly grease a baking sheet with an oil or shortening. Then dump your nut/seeds into a bowl. Add in the flax meal mixture you just made, stirring to coat the nuts. Pour the remaining ingredients on top and stir to combine. Spread onto the baking sheet in an even layer and pop 'em into the oven. Bake for an hour, stirring every 20 minutes or so. Let cool and enjoy!

Funky Options:

- 1/2 tsp of any of the following in place of the cinnamon: rosemary, thyme, cayenne pepper, sage, or oregano

Substitutions

Sometimes you come across ingredients you had never given much attention until you started cooking for someone with food allergies. Baking powder, eggs, or soy sauce are a few of mine. This is a list of my favorite substitutions for common products you may need to replace in cooking for someone with food allergies.

Baking Powder

Ingredients:

Equal parts Cream of Tartar and Baking Soda

Eggs

For 1 Whole Egg in Baked Goods:

- 1/4 cup Fruit or Veggie Puree

For 1 Egg White:

- Stir in 2 tablespoons flaxseed meal into 1/4 cup water over medium heat. Bring to a boil; continue stirring until it becomes the consistency of egg whites.

Chicken Stock

Discovering that Landon was allergic to carrots pretty much eliminated all store-bought chicken stock. So I was grateful my mother-in-law knew how to make it from scratch. Even though Landon can eat carrots now, I still make our chicken stock because it saves us money and I love the feeling of making something out of nothing!

Ingredients:

- Chicken Carcass (Roast a whole chicken and use the meat for a couple meals, then save the bones to make your stock)
- Vegetables (Celery, Onions, Garlic, Carrots, Fennel, etc.)

Place chicken carcass and veggies into large Crockpot, and cover with water. Place lid on Crockpot, set to high and leave overnight or at least 8 hours. Then strain the gorgeous golden chicken stock through a strainer or sieve to remove the bones and vegetables. Pour into quart-sized freezer Ziploc bags. Lay flat in your freezer.

Funky Options:

- Freeze in silicone muffin liners. Once frozen, pop out, and store in gallon-sized freezer bags. This makes perfect 1/4 cup chicken stock portions. Great for cooking with!

Corn-Free Corn Syrup

There are certain recipes you can't make without good ol' corn syrup—fudge, marshmallows, and Rice Krispies Treats come to mind. This is also perfect for pecan pies and candy!

Ingredients:

- 2 c. Sugar
- 3/4 c. Water
- 1/4 tsp. Cream of Tartar
- 1/8 tsp. Salt
- Candy Thermometer

In a big saucepan with a lid, combine the ingredients, and bring them to a boil. Reduce heat until you reach a simmer, cover for 3 minutes. Uncover and cook until it reaches "soft-ball" stage, about 240 degrees. Cook and store in the fridge.

Marshmallows

For the record, you can live without marshmallows. They don't contain anything nutritionally important or beneficial for that matter. But can you really live without Rice Crispy Treats and Fudge? Of this I am not altogether convinced—which is why I have a Funky Food friendly marshmallow recipe. You can either make these completely into marshmallows or leave it as fluff for your Rice Crispy Treat craving!

Ingredients:

- 4 pks. Unflavored Gelatin (3 Tbsp. plus 1 1/2 tsp.)
- 3 c. Sugar
- 1 1/4 c. Corn-Free Corn Syrup (page 199)
- 1/4 tsp. Salt
- 2 tsp. Vanilla Extract
- 1 1/2 c. Corn-Free Powdered Sugar (page 209)
- Candy Thermometer

Oil a 9x13 baking dish with canola oil, then line it with parchment paper allowing about 2 inches to drape over the sides, then oil the parchment paper. Trust me, marshmallows are sticky—you want to oil everything. Toss sugar, corn-free corn syrup (page 199), salt, and 3/4 cup water into a saucepan. Stir to dissolve the sugar while bringing to a boil over high heat. Stop stirring and let the temperature reach 238 degrees. While it's cooking, put 3/4 cup cold water into your stand mixer and add the gelatin. Let it stand for about 5 minutes. Using your whisk attachment, combine the syrup mixture with the gelatin. Beat on high until it's really stiff—this will take awhile, maybe 10 minutes or more. Add in the vanilla. Stop here if you only need marshmallow fluff.

For Marshmallows:

Pour mixture into your well-oiled, parchment-lined dish and smooth. Let cool until firm, about 3 hours. "Flour" your countertop with some of your Homemade Powdered Sugar. Turn your newly made marshmallows onto the countertop, and yank off the parchment paper. Using an oiled knife or cookie cutters, cut the marshmallows into your desired shape. Roll each marshmallow in more of the Homemade Powdered Sugar. These will stay gorgeous for about 3 days, so eat 'em up!

Nut/Seed Butter

Why would a cookbook about food allergies include so much information about nut/seed butters? Mainly because only about 2% of the population is allergic to tree nuts and even then that leaves plenty of nuts and seeds to choose from. They are a great source of protein, work fantastic in rotation diets, most have omega-3s and kids love them. All good things when you are dealing with food allergies!

Ingredients:

- 2 c. Nut/Seed of Choice
- Several Tbsp. Matching Oil of Choice

Simply toss nuts/seeds into a food processor and start pureeing. Then, drizzle oil, one tablespoon at a time into the food processor until you have smooth but thick nut/seed butter.

Here are my favorite combinations:

- Almonds and Almond Oil
- Brazil Nuts and Oil of Choice
- Cashews and Oil of Choice
- Hazelnuts and Hazelnut Oil
- Hemp Seeds and Hemp Oil
- Macadamia Nuts and Macadamia Oil

- Roasted Pumpkin Seeds and Oil of Choice

- Pecans and Pecan Oil

- Pine Nuts and Oil of Choice

- Pistachios and Oil of Choice

- Sunflower Seeds and Sunflower Seed Oil

- Walnuts and Walnut Oil

If you can't find one of these oils then use canola, grape seed, or olive oil. Avoid using extra virgin olive oil; it has a strong flavor.

Nut/Seed/Grain Milk

Just like the nut/seed butters, almost any nut/seed and even some grains can be turned into milk. Milks are great for baking and adding nutrients into recipes for anyone needing a little extra something in their diet! Since we use so much of these milks, I purchased a Soyabella Milk Machine. It easily paid for itself in the money we saved from buying these milks at the store.

Ingredients:

Here are my favorite Nut/Seed/Grain Milks:

- Almonds
- Brazil Nuts
- Cashews
- Hazelnuts
- Hemp Seeds
- Macadamia Nuts
- Roasted Pumpkin Seeds
- Oat
- Pecans
- Pine Nuts
- Pistachios

- Rice
- Sunflower Seeds
- Walnuts

Tip: Feel free to add a few tablespoons of a liquid sweeteners or salt to your milks. Most store purchased milks have!

Papaya

I couldn't chat up a papaya in my Super Smoothie (page 189) and then leave you with no information on what a ripe one looks like or how to prepare it, could I? This will save you from the potentially embarrassing moment at the natural foods store when you are busted by the produce clerk for manhandling a papaya. Like he's never over-handled fresh produce.

A ripe papaya is mostly yellow-orange in color, soft, and smells great. Don't bother buying a green one hoping it will ripen. It won't.

Preparation:

After washing it, slice the papaya in half, and scoop out the black seeds. Chew a couple seeds before a meal to help get those digestive enzymes flowing. I wouldn't try this with a kid though. Papaya seeds are black and slimy. On second thought, a kid might dig that.

Papaya skin is really thin. Slice it off with about 1/8 inch of fruit with it.

Storage:

Dice up and eat, blend, or freeze for later. If you are going to freeze it, place it on a baking sheet first. Then place it in the freezer to freeze completely. Finally, toss them into freezer bags. If you dump them into freezer bags without freezing them first, you'll have a large glob of papaya that will require a pickax to disassemble. Not that I did this. More than once.

Powdered Sugar (Corn-Free)

Powdered sugar is one of those ingredients that I'm not terribly sure why we ever stopped making it ourselves. It's crazy easy to make and only takes a few minutes. It's also in that category of products that contains corn. Powdered sugar is a must when making frosting for those 5 dozen cupcakes you baked for all your kiddo's birthday buddies!

Ingredients:

- 1 c. Sugar
- 1 Tbsp. Tapioca Starch

Place in blender, food processor, or Vitamix. Blend for one minute. Yup, that's it. You will magically have powdered sugar. You mad cooking magician, you!

Funky Options:

Try using any starch in place of the tapioca or try out some sugar alternatives!

Desserts

After the bread section, this was the first place you came. Tell the truth. Desserts become very important once you are faced with your very first allergen-free birthday. Looking at your child's face and realizing that you are going to have to make cupcakes or cookies out of ingredients most people have never heard of is intimidating! There are plenty of simple and delicious options here to help you bring a huge smile to your child's face. Don't forget, if all else fails, use some of your homemade powdered sugar and frost a muffin. Muffins really are cupcakes in disguise, after all.

Almond Blueberry Cookie Bars

This recipe was created on Almond/Blueberry/Buckwheat Day when Landon was on the rotation diet. They turned out delicious and now are a staple in my dessert favorites.

Ingredients:

- 1 c. Almond Meal
- 1 c. Buckwheat Flour
- 2/3 c. Brown Sugar
- 1/4 tsp. Baking Soda
- 1 c. Almond Butter or Regular Butter
- 1 c. All-Fruit Jam (or Fruit Filling Recipe below)

Preheat oven to 350 degrees. Combine the dry ingredients and mix together. Using a pastry blender or a couple of knives, cut 3/4 cup of almond butter into the flour mixture. Reserve 1/2 cup of the crumb mixture. Press remaining mixture into a greased 9x2x2 inch baking pan. Spread out the fruit filling or jam over the top. Using the pastry blender, cut remaining almond butter into reserved mixture. It should resemble coarse crumbs. Sprinkle over the top of the fruit filling. Bake for 30-35 minutes or until topping is golden brown. Let cool, slice, and serve.

Fruit Filling Recipe

In a saucepan, combine 10 ounces of fruit, 2 tablespoons of water, 1 tablespoon lemon juice, apple cider vinegar, and spices like cinnamon if you want. Bring to a boil and reduce heat. Simmer uncovered for about 8 minutes or until fruit is tender and you have a nice thick sauce.

Funky Options:

- Almond Meal/Butter Substitutions: Pecan, Hemp Seed, Walnut, or Sunflower Seed Meal/Butter

- Buckwheat Flour Substitution: Sorghum, Oat, or Amaranth

Almond Cookies

Creating these cookies was a great moment in my cooking history. I realized that nut butters function almost like regular butter in baked goods. I can't quite explain the joy this brought to a dairy/soy-free mama's heart! Plus, I loved the idea of finding yet another way to get more omega-3s into my family members. This cookie is chewy yet crunchy. You're going to love 'em!

Ingredients:

- 3/4 c. Almond Butter
- 1/2 c. Sugar
- 1/2 c. Brown Sugar
- 1/4 c. Applesauce (or any fruit puree)
- 1 tsp. Vanilla (or keep with the theme and try almond extract)
- 1/4 tsp. Cream of Tartar
- 1/4 tsp. Baking Soda
- 1 1/2 c. Almond Meal
- 1/2 tsp. Cinnamon
- 1/4 tsp. Nutmeg
- 1/4 tsp. Salt
- Turbinado Sugar for rolling

Preheat oven to 350 degrees. Cream almond butter and sugars together. Add in applesauce and vanilla. Blend in almond meal and remaining ingredients. This dough should be cookie dough consistency but will be sticky. Roll teaspoon size balls with your hands and then roll them in turbinado sugar. Place on a Silpat lined baking sheet and press with fork to flatten out a little. Bake for 8 minutes or until browned around the edges.

Funky Options:

- Almond Butter Substitution: Any nut/seed butter will work. Try walnuts, pecans, sunflower seeds, or hazelnuts.

- Almond Meal Substitution: Use 2 cups walnut (or any nut/seed) in place of the 1 1/2 cups Almond Meal. (Not a typo—the almond meal is lower in fat than just about any other nut/seed, so you need more of the alternatives to make the dough work.)

Buckwheat Hemp Butter Cookies

If you are craving peanut butter cookies, these work great. The combination of buckwheat and hemp butter has a very peanut buttery taste along with the wonderful chewy but sandy nature of a true peanut butter cookie.

Ingredients:

- 3/4 c. Hemp Butter
- 1/2 c. Sugar
- 1/2 c. Brown Sugar
- 1/4 c. Applesauce
- 1 tsp. Vanilla
- 1/4 tsp. Cream of Tartar
- 1/4 tsp. Baking Soda
- 1 1/2 c. Buckwheat Flour
- 1/4 tsp. Salt

Preheat oven to 350 degrees. Mix together hemp butter and sugars. Add in remaining ingredients and blend. Slowly add in 1 1/2 cups buckwheat flour and 1/4 tsp salt. Combine together. Drop teaspoonfuls onto Silpat-lined baking sheet, slide them into the oven and bake for 8 minutes. Let cool slightly and enjoy!

Funky Options:

- Hemp Butter Substitutions: Use any seed/nut butter but it will alter the flavor of the cookies slightly. Hemp Butter has a very mild flavor.

- Buckwheat Flour Substitution: 1 cup Rice Flour and 1/2 cup Starch, or 1 cup Sorghum Flour and 1/2 cup Starch

- Press onto the Tops: SunDrops or Dairy-Free Chocolate Chips

Crispy Treats/Cake

These were one of the first recipes I ever learned how to make as a child. Now Landon and I can make them too! I hope you and your family have as much fun with this as we do. These can easily be shaped into a gorgeous cake for an allergen-free birthday cake!

Ingredients:

- 1/4 c. Coconut Oil
- 1 c. Homemade Marshmallow Fluff
- 5 c. Crispy Rice Cereal

Melt Coconut Oil in a large saucepan over medium heat. Add in the homemade marshmallow fluff and stir to combine. Remove from heat and stir in Crispy Rice Cereal. Pour onto parchment paper. Let cool and cut into desired shapes.

Crispy Cake

Oil two cake pans. Pour the hot Crispy Treat mixture into each pan. Press lightly into pan. Let cool and using a knife to loosen, dump out crispy cake onto a cake plate. Use some of your homemade icing to finish off this fun birthday cake!

Funky Options:

- Crispy Rice Cereal Substitutions: Puffed Millet, Puffed Amaranth, or any Crunchy Cereal that fits your needs
- Add any of the following: Chopped Pecans, SunDrops, or Dairy-free Chocolate Chips

Oat Flour Cupcakes

I felt like one of the three bears from the children's classic while getting this recipe right. The first batch was too dense. The second not sweet enough. I was down to my last 3 Tablespoons of coconut oil when the finally came out just right.

Ingredients:

- 1 1/2 cups Oat Flour
- 1/2 cup Rice Flour
- 1 cup Sugar
- 1/2 tsp Salt
- 1 tsp Cream of Tartar
- 2 tsp Baking Soda
- 1 T Ener-G Egg Replacer
- 1 cup Coconut Milk
- 3 T Kelapo Coconut Oil
- 1 T Vanilla
- 1/4 tsp vinegar

Preheat your oven to 350 degrees. Line your muffin tin with cupcake liners. Whisk together your dry ingredients. Normally I'm pretty lazy about this step, but you really need the ingredients evenly spread out. Toss in the wet ingredients and beat the snot out of 'em until you have a gorgeous, smooth batter. Fill up the cupcake liners about 3/4 of the way. Bake for about 20 minutes or until a toothpick comes out clean and the tops are slightly golden. Let cool completely before you ice them with this:

Cupcake Icing

- 1 pound Corn-free Powdered Sugar
- 1/4 cup Coconut Milk

Blend ingredients. This makes a thinner icing, definitely not a buttercream. I like it because it gives the cupcake a little something without reducing it to being simply the carrier of the icing.

Hot Chocolate

One of Landon's Preschool Teachers thought it would be fun for the kids to have a cup of hot chocolate at school. One of the many things that make having a kid with food allergies a challenge! Up to this point we had been simply making hot chocolate with whatever milk he was drinking. But he needed a powdered version to take to school. This recipe is a snap and would make a great holiday gift for a family coping with food allergies!

Ingredients:

- 3 Tbsp. Sugar

- 1 Tbsp. Cocoa or Carob

- 1/4 c. Powdered Non-Dairy Milk

Combine dry ingredients. Store in an airtight container. To make hot cocoa, add one cup of hot water, stir, and serve!

Funky Options:

Try the "Better Than Milk" Powdered Rice Milk for this recipe.

Icing

Icing is important. Just ask any kid facing a birthday cupcake without it, and they will tell you. Every child deserves a cupcake loaded with inches of this creamy goodness!

Ingredients:

- 2 Tbsp. Coconut Oil
- 1 c. Corn-Free Powdered Sugar
- 1/2 c. Rice Milk
- 2 tsp. Vanilla

Alright, I'll admit it, I wing making icing. Cream the Coconut Oil, add in the vanilla, toss in the powdered sugar then start drizzling in the milk. Stop adding milk when you have a gorgeous, creamy icing!

Funky Options:

- Add any of the following: 4 tablespoons Cocoa Powder, 1/4 cup Strawberry Puree (add extra powdered sugar), 2 teaspoons Cinnamon, or 1 teaspoon Nutmeg

Lollipops

Once again it was school that prodded me out of my pajamas and into trying recipes that wouldn't have even crossed my stovetop. Sure, I bought the healthier version of lollipops at my favorite health food store, but make my own? To my sincere relief, I discovered candy making is a cinch. Enjoy!

Ingredients:

- 2 c. Granulated Sugar
- 2/3 c. Honey
- 3/4 c. Water
- Food Coloring or 1/4 c. Beet Juice (pour it out of a can of beets)
- Olive Oil or Glycerin for greasing molds
- Candy Flavoring (optional)
- Hard Candy Molds
- Lollipop Sticks
- Candy Thermometer

Use some olive oil or glycerin to grease up your molds, and place your lollipop sticks in the molds. Attach candy thermometer to the side of your large saucepan with the tip **not** *touching the bottom of the pan*. In the saucepan, mix together sugar, honey, and water. Stir over medium heat until sugar dissolves. Bring mixture to a boil without stirring. When syrup temperature reaches 260 degrees F, add food coloring or beet juice. Remove from heat at 300 degrees. After boiling ceases, you can add flavoring and stir. A word of caution: it is almost impossible to cover up the flavor of honey in this recipe. If you want a different flavored lollipop use the Corn-Free Corn Syrup in place of the honey. Pour syrup into the lightly oiled candy molds. When cooled, pop out of the molds, and dip into sugar to prevent sticking. Store in an airtight container or wrap in individual plastic candy bags (check your favorite craft store).

Funky Options:

- Substitute Corn-Free Corn Syrup (page 199), Agave Nectar, or Brown Rice Syrup

No-Bake Cookies

This childhood staple is a must for any household. Plus it meets my requirements for a Funky Food recipe: it's simple, versatile, and delicious!

Bring to a Boil for 1 minute:

- 1/2 c. Butter or Coconut Oil

- 2 c. Sugar

- 1/4 c. Cocoa or Carob Powder (optional)

- 1/2 c. Milk of Choice

- Take off heat and stir in:

- 1 tsp. Vanilla

- 1/2 c. Nut/Seed Butter of Choice

- 3 c. Gluten-free Oats

- Drop teaspoonfuls onto wax paper. Let cool and eat!

Funky Options:

- Milk Suggestions: Coconut, Rice, Hemp, Almond, etc

- Nut/Seed Butters Suggestions: Sunflower Seed, Almond, or Hemp

- Oats Substitutions: Quinoa Flakes, Puffed Millet, or Cooked Rice

Oatmeal Cookies

A lot of my great recipes start from cookbooks. It reminds me of using a pattern to make a dress, but choosing unique material, thread, and accessories. Rotation diets are challenging for many reasons, but finding allergy friendly recipes that fit is almost impossible. So, I was very excited that these single grain cookies worked so well.

Ingredients:

- 1 3/4 c. Oat Flour
- 2 tsp. Baking Soda
- 1 tsp. Cream of Tartar
- 1/2 tsp. Salt
- 1/2 tsp. Cinnamon
- 1/2 tsp. Nutmeg
- 2 c. Coconut Oil
- 1 1/2 c. Packed Brown Sugar
- 1/4 c. Sugar
- 1/2 c. Applesauce
- 2 1/2 tsp. Vanilla
- 3 1/2 c. Oatmeal

Preheat oven to 350 and pull out those Silpat-lined baking sheets. Cream together your wet ingredients. Toss in the dry, saving the oats for last. Drop in teaspoonfuls onto Silpat-lined or greased baking sheets. Bake for about 10 minutes or until golden brown. They will be fragile so let cool slightly before removing to a rack to cool completely.

Funky Options:

- Substitute Applesauce with any fruit or vegetable puree.

- Add any of the following: 1/2 cup Dairy-free Chocolate Chips, 1/2 cup chopped Pecans, or 1/2 cup Raisins.

Pudding

Puddings are great for kids with food allergies. They are so versatile! You can use any nut/seed milk and any grain or not use a grain and enjoy a creamy, delicious dessert.

Ingredients:

- 2 c. Cooked Quinoa (try making this in your rice maker)
- 4 c. Hemp Milk
- 1/2 c. Sugar
- 1/2 tsp. Vanilla (optional)

In a sauce pan, combine milk, sugar, and cocoa powder and whisk until combined. Add cooked quinoa. Cook uncovered for 30-40 minutes over medium heat, stirring frequently. The pudding is done when the quinoa and milk make a thick porridge. Remove from heat, and stir in vanilla. Spoon into a bowl and serve warm or refrigerate.

Funky Options:

- Quinoa Substitutions: Cooked Rice, Millet, or Buckwheat
- Hemp Milk Substitutions: Rice, Oat, Coconut, Almond, or Sunflower Seed
- Add any of the following: 2 tablespoons Cocoa Powder or Carob Powder, 2 teaspoons Cinnamon, or 1/2 teaspoon Nutmeg